Did Microsoft Harm Consumers?

T0272906

Did Microsoft Harm Consumers?

Two Opposing Views

David S. Evans
Franklin M. Fisher
Daniel L. Rubinfeld
Richard L. Schmalensee

AEI-Brookings Joint Center for Regulatory Studies

WASHINGTON, D.C.

2000

To order call toll free 1-800-462-6420 or 1-717-794-3800. For all other inquiries please contact the AEI Press, 1150 Seventeenth Street, N.W., Washington, D.C. 20036 or call 1-800-862-5801.

ISBN 0-8447-7151-1
ISBN 978-0-8447-7151-9
3 5 7 9 10 8 6 4 2

The AEI Press
Publisher for the American Enterprise Institute
1150 17th Street, N.W.
Washington, D.C. 20036

Contents

FOREWORD, *Robert W. Hahn and Robert E. Litan* vii

1 *UNITED STATES V. MICROSOFT:* AN ECONOMIC ANALYSIS 1
   Franklin M. Fisher and Daniel L. Rubinfeld

2 BE NICE TO YOUR RIVALS: HOW THE GOVERNMENT
   IS SELLING AN ANTITRUST CASE WITHOUT
   CONSUMER HARM IN *UNITED STATES V. MICROSOFT* 45
   David S. Evans and Richard L. Schmalensee

3 MISCONCEPTIONS, MISDIRECTION, AND MISTAKES 87
   Franklin M. Fisher and Daniel L. Rubinfeld

4 CONSUMERS LOSE IF LEADING FIRMS ARE SMASHED
   FOR COMPETING 97
   David S. Evans and Richard L. Schmalensee

   APPENDIX 107

   NOTES 109

   ABOUT THE AUTHORS 133

Foreword

United States v. Microsoft is arguably "the" antitrust case of the past decade. It will have important implications for how governments regulate information technologies and the coming Internet explosion. It will also have important consequences for how businesses behave in the marketplace and in the political arena.

Because the *Microsoft* case has captured the attention of the public and the press, we thought that it would be useful to provide an informed assessment of the economic and policy issues underlying the case. Typically, the AEI-Brookings Joint Center commissions studies from academics who do not have a direct stake in the issue under study. In this volume we decided to take a different tack. We asked the leading economists on the government side of the case and the Microsoft side of the case to lay out their views on the key issues and then to respond to the views presented by the opposing side. We did so because we felt that the leading economists would have access to information that outsiders might not easily obtain. We also felt that readers would then be in a good position to reach their own conclusions about the case.

We hope that this volume will highlight the fundamental areas of agreement and disagreement on this case. We also hope that this volume will illuminate many of the complex issues involved in assessing the appropriate scope for antitrust intervention in information technology industries.

ROBERT W. HAHN
ROBERT E. LITAN
AEI-Brookings Joint Center
for Regulatory Studies

1

United States v. *Microsoft:* An Economic Analysis

Franklin M. Fisher and
Daniel L. Rubinfeld

In May 1998, the U.S. Department of Justice, claiming a number of violations of Sections 1 and 2 of the Sherman Act, filed suit against the Microsoft Corporation.[1] The case was tried in the U.S. District Court of the District of Columbia from October 19, 1998, through June 24, 1999. Judge Thomas Penfield Jackson ruled as to the findings of fact on November 5, 1999. As this chapter is drafted, the parties have prepared briefs on proposed conclusions of law and are involved in settlement discussions. If the parties reach no settlement and Judge Jackson rules in favor of the Department of Justice, remedy issues will then come into play.

This chapter presents perspective and commentary on the economic issues from the viewpoint of two economists who were active in the case. Franklin M. Fisher was one of the U.S. government's economic witnesses at the trial, and this chapter is based in part on his testimony. Daniel L. Rubinfeld was deputy assistant attorney general for economics in the Antitrust Division during much of the investigation. During the trial he was deputy assistant attorney general and later a consultant for the U.S. government.

1

Our roles as testifying expert and chief economist at the Antitrust Division, respectively, carry with them the advantage of seeing the issues from the inside as participants and the disadvantage that one's perspective is inevitably affected by one's own viewpoint. Because our goal is to explicate the merits of the government's case and to highlight important issues, we hope that the advantages will outweigh any disadvantages.[2]

Summary of Opinions

Microsoft raises three basic economic questions. First, did the Microsoft Corporation possess monopoly power in the market for personal computer operating systems? Second, did Microsoft maintain its monopoly power by anticompetitive conduct? Finally, did Microsoft use its monopoly power in an anticompetitive way to distort competition or achieve monopoly power in markets other than the market or markets for personal computer operating systems?

In general, a violation of Section 2 of the Sherman Act requires both the possession of monopoly power and its acquisition or maintenance by acts not consistent with competitive profit-maximizing behavior. Our answer to the three central questions is that Microsoft achieved monopoly power in the market for operating systems for Intel-compatible desktop personal computers. In addition, Microsoft foresaw the possibility that the dominant position of its Windows operating system would be eroded by Internet browsers and by cross-platform Java, which are capable of supporting software applications that are independent of the operating system. Microsoft therefore took anticompetitive actions that were ultimately successful to exclude competition in Internet browsers so as to protect the current dominance of its Windows operating system. In protecting that dominance, Microsoft also took anticompetitive actions to restrain the use and availability of the cross-platform Java technology. Further, Microsoft

engaged in a number of anticompetitive acts and solicitations designed to convince other firms not to compete against Microsoft in platform-level software.

Microsoft's conduct included a number of actions to preserve and increase barriers to entry into the PC operating system market. First, the firm tied its browser to the operating system—in effect requiring manufacturers to acquire its Internet browser as a condition of acquiring its Windows operating system. As a result, Microsoft severely hampered Netscape in browser competition and blunted the threat that software developers, writing for a browser platform, would write a platform not under Microsoft's control.[3] Second, Microsoft excluded browser competitors from the most efficient channels of distribution and thus required competitors to use more costly and less efficient channels. Third, the firm imposed agreements requiring original equipment manufacturers not to remove Microsoft's browser or to substitute an alternative browser. Fourth, Microsoft imposed agreements on online services, Internet service providers, and Internet content providers that required them to boycott or disfavor Netscape and other browsers. Those agreements prohibited online services from promoting, distributing, using, or paying for Netscape's browser, or allowed them to do so only on less-favored terms, and thereby further excluded competition. Fifth, Microsoft gave its browser away for free—committing itself to do so "forever"—and, indeed, paid others to take its browser. Finally, Microsoft contained the cross-platform threat of Java by growing "polluted" Java, designed to entrap software developers into writing Java programs that would not run except with Windows.

The principal effect of Microsoft's anticompetitive conduct was the maintenance of the firm's operating systems monopoly. Absent an appropriate remedy, platforms that do not use a Microsoft standard will not prosper, and a critical opportunity for innovation that reduces or eliminates Microsoft's power will have been lost.

Further, to the extent that Microsoft is unchecked in its anticompetitive actions, the incentive of other firms to innovate in areas competitive with Microsoft will be reduced. Thus, if software developers believe that Microsoft will engage in anticompetitive acts to impede any innovation that threatens its monopoly, they will have substantially reduced incentives to innovate in competition with Microsoft. As a result, consumers have a limited range of software products from which to choose, and that limited choice reduces consumer welfare.

What the Case Was Not About. It is important to highlight what the case was *not* about. First, the government did not file the suit because Microsoft was innovative. Indeed, the case was not brought because Microsoft's innovations happened to bring with them monopoly power. The government filed the case because Microsoft took anticompetitive actions to maintain that power—actions that were not separately profitable innovations, but rather actions that prevented competitive innovations from getting a fair market trial.

Second, some commentators have expressed the view that the risk of inappropriate antitrust enforcement is excessive in an innovative, dynamic industry such as computer software. To the contrary, we believe that because of the central and essential role the personal computer operating system plays, and is expected to play, in both commercial and consumer endeavors—including access to the Internet and the World Wide Web—the costs of improperly maintaining monopoly power over the operating system, and the danger that Microsoft will use its existing monopoly power to monopolize other critical markets linked to the operating system, were and are very great.

For example, to the extent that Internet browsers or Java, or both, in fact threatened and indeed actually undermined Microsoft's operating system monopoly (by eroding the applications barrier to entry protecting that monopoly), substantial economic costs arise from permitting Microsoft to rebuild that barrier to entry through the stifling of non-Microsoft browsers and cross-platform Java and, more generally, platform innovations that threaten Microsoft.

Third, *Microsoft* was not a case about bundling any two products so as to leverage an existing monopoly. The government did not claim that Microsoft attempted to use its existing monopoly power over PC operating systems to monopolize the market for Internet browsers for its own sake. Rather, the government claimed that Microsoft's goal was to maintain its operating systems monopoly. If it were successful in achieving that goal, the economic costs to consumers and the economy would be substantial.

Finally, a number of commentators have suggested that the government's case was weak or incomplete because it failed to show immediate consumer harm. In fact, the government did present evidence of immediate harm, which we spell out later in this chapter. In any case, we disagree with those commentators for a number of reasons. First, antitrust law does not require proof of such harm. The law merely requires proof of harm to competition on the general presumption that such harm, in turn, leads to harm to consumers. Second, to require such proof would be to immunize any predatory practice. For example, during a predatory pricing campaign, the predatorily low price benefits consumers; the harm comes in the resulting effects on competition. That point goes beyond pricing. In dynamic, innovative industries, initial consumer benefits can lead to later consumer harm if the improper use of monopoly power adversely affects the pattern of product innovation, pricing, and quality. Third, the fact that innovation can bring consumer benefits should not provide a license for innovative firms to engage in anticompetitive acts.

We begin our analysis by laying out some basic issues relating to the economics of PC operating systems and applications, after which we concentrate on the antitrust implications of a number of Microsoft's actions.

The Economics of Competition and Monopoly

Market power is the ability of a seller of a product profitably to maintain prices above competitive levels. Monopoly power is a substantial degree of market power. While a firm with a slight degree of market power may find it profitable to charge supranormal prices for a short time or to charge prices that are only slightly supranormal, a firm with monopoly power will find it profitable to charge a price significantly in excess of competitive levels and to do so over a significant period of time.

It is important to stress that success achieved through legitimate means such as innovation, superior marketing, or historical accident may naturally give rise to market power or even monopoly power. The very fact that the software industry is so innovative, together with its immense and growing importance in the American economy, makes it crucial that success be restricted to success on the merits and that monopoly power be confined to that which results from such success. Even a firm that has attained monopoly power through legitimate means and natural economic effects must not be permitted to retain or extend that power through artificial, anticompetitive means.

Our analysis of competition and monopoly in *Microsoft* involves four key questions: How does one identify monopoly power? What is the role of network effects? What is an anticompetitive act? How can a firm with monopoly power in one market use that power to gain advantages in other markets in ways that are anticompetitive and serve to protect or extend the firm's power in the first market?

How Does One Identify Monopoly Power? The hallmark of monopoly power is the absence or ineffectiveness of competitive constraints on price, output, product decisions, and quality. One usually addresses the issue of monopoly power by defining "the relevant market" and assessing shares in that market. That is at least a beginning guide to the presence or absence of market power and a way of organizing the facts that one will have to take into account. Because the purpose of defining the relevant market is to identify monopoly power, if it exists, the "relevant market" should include all those products that reasonably serve to constrain the behavior of the alleged monopolist. Such constraints arise from three sources: substitution by consumers to other products (demand substitutability), substitution by producers to other products (supply substitutability), and entry of new productive capacity.

Scholars, analysts, and policymakers have long recognized these principles. Since 1982, the Department of Justice's *Merger Guidelines* have approached market definition in merger cases by asking in part whether a single, profit-maximizing firm controlling a candidate market could raise price from the *prevailing* level by a significant amount (5 percent) for a nonnegligible time period.[4] When the issue is instead whether a particular firm possesses market power or monopoly power, it is necessary to consider raising price *from the competitive level.*[5]

Having defined an appropriate market, one then goes on to consider market share and the ability of firms not in the market to enter in the event of an attempt by the alleged monopolist to earn supranormal profits through an exercise of power. A key distinguishing feature of monopoly power is its durability. If entry would rapidly frustrate a firm's attempt to earn supranormal profits by pricing above competitive levels, that firm does not possess monopoly power.

Barriers to entry are factors that would prevent entry in the face of supranormal profits. Those factors also limit the expansion of existing firms. Where significant barriers to entry exist, monopoly power can be present; otherwise, it cannot.

What Is the Role of Network Effects? The barriers to entry in the present case stem from a combination of economies of scale and network effects. Like all software, applications programming exhibits substantial economies of scale, because most of the costs come in the creation of the software and are independent of the number of copies produced. Hence, software developers wish to write for operating systems or other platforms that have a large number of users.

Network effects arise when the attractiveness of a product to customers increases with the use of that product by others. Indeed, the fact that many applications are written for a given operating system and cannot easily run on other operating systems makes that operating system more attractive to users. Interestingly, before *Microsoft*, the importance of the availability of applications for operating systems networks has been unappreciated.[6]

Taken together, those network effects and scale economies create a positive feedback: the more users an operating system has, the more applications will be written for it; the more applications written for an operating system, the more users it will acquire. After that feedback effect has operated for a while, it becomes difficult or impossible for a new operating system to make much of an inroad.

In such circumstances, it is natural for one firm to become dominant in operating systems and thus to acquire monopoly power. But the fact that the successful firm has acquired monopoly power with a "natural" barrier to entry does not justify its taking anticompetitive actions to extend that power to another market or, in particular, its engaging in anticompetitive acts that serve to buttress and protect its power in the original market.[7]

What Is an Anticompetitive Act? In the case of a single firm, anticompetitive acts typically involve the taking of measures that are more restrictive of competition than necessary. In our view, a predatory anticompetitive act is an act that is

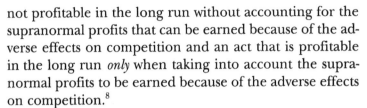

not profitable in the long run without accounting for the supranormal profits that can be earned because of the adverse effects on competition and an act that is profitable in the long run *only* when taking into account the supranormal profits to be earned because of the adverse effects on competition.[8]

In effect, a predatory anticompetitive act is one that involves a deliberate sacrifice of profit to secure or protect monopoly power. A firm that takes an action not expected to be profit-maximizing, save for the monopoly rents that stem from the act's effects on competition, is using its assets in a way that incurs an opportunity cost—a sacrifice of the profits that the firm could have made had it instead taken a profit-maximizing action.[9] If the firm does that to earn supranormal profits dependent on the effects of its actions on competition, then that firm has taken an action that is not profitable except for those effects and is anticompetitive.[10]

Economic Analysis of Microsoft's Actions

Monopoly Power. Microsoft possesses monopoly power in the market for operating systems for Intel-compatible desktop personal computers.[11] Evidence presented in *Microsoft* showed that for the past few years, and for the reasonably foreseeable future, there were and will be no reasonable substitutes for Microsoft's Windows operating systems for Intel-compatible desktop PCs. For example, numerous representatives from PC original equipment manufacturers— the most important direct customers for PC operating systems—testified that original equipment manufacturers do not believe that they have any alternative to the acquisition and installation of Microsoft's Windows operating system. They would continue to take Windows even at a 10 percent price increase and did take it, even though some of them vigorously objected to the restrictions that Microsoft imposed on them.[12] For example, John Romano of Hewlett Packard wrote to Microsoft that "if we had another supplier, I guarantee you would not be our supplier of choice."[13]

Microsoft's share of personal computer operating systems is very high and has remained stable over time. Microsoft's worldwide share of shipments of Intel-based operating systems had been approximately 90 percent or more in recent years.[14]

It is instructive to note that the existence of Apple does not much affect Microsoft's monopoly power. Although new users—and perhaps some existing ones—choose between PCs and Apple machines, a substantial increase in the price of Windows, say 10 percent, corresponds to only a small increase in the price of a PC and will make few, if any, users switch. Moreover, *Microsoft* is about operating systems, not PCs; it is irrelevant whether a separate market for PCs even exists.

Looking forward, for similar reasons, the possibility that nondesktop devices such as the Palm Pilot may partially substitute for the PC instead of remaining a complement to it also does not limit Microsoft's monopoly power. Even if such substitution were to become important—and that is doubtful—it would merely make Microsoft's monopoly less important; it would not make the monopoly disappear.

In any event, even if non-Intel-based machines are included in the operating system market, Microsoft's share has been high and stable, since Apple accounts for only about 12 percent of all personal computers. Moreover, while Microsoft's high market share is indicative of its monopoly power, the direct evidence of the original equipment manufacturers shows the existence of that power, and the analysis of barriers to entry confirms it.

As mentioned above, operating systems are characterized by network effects. Users want an operating system that will permit them to run all the applications programs they want to use; developers tend to write applications for the most popular operating system; and applications software written for a specific operating system cannot run on a different operating system without extensive and costly modifications or add-ons. Operating systems provide applications programming interfaces through which applications interact with the operating system, and through the operating system with the computer hardware. Applications developers must write their programs to interact with a particular operating system's applications programming interfaces. The time and expense of then "porting" the applications to a different operating system can be substantial. An applications programming interface set to which applications may be written is often referred to in the industry as a "platform."

Other network effects exist. For example, operating systems are complex; they exhibit network effects in part because firms are reluctant to invest in retraining workers and in part because using multiple operating systems vastly increases technical support costs. Thus, firms have an incentive to have the same operating systems for all their own computers and the same operating system that is widely used by other firms. Other network effects include the ease of exchanging files and the opportunity to learn from others.

As the result of economies of scale and network effects, Microsoft's high market share has led to many more applications being written for its operating system than for any other. That has reinforced and increased Microsoft's market share and thus has led to still more applications being written for Windows than for other operating systems, and so on. That positive feedback effect—the applications barrier to entry—has made it difficult or impossible for rival operating systems to compete effectively with Microsoft by gaining more than a niche in the market. New entry is not likely to erode Microsoft's market share and market power as long as the applications barrier to entry remains strong—a conclusion also supported by Microsoft's internal documents and other evidence.[15]

Substantial evidence showed that Microsoft did not consider other operating system vendors as a material constraint on its current pricing of the Windows operating system.[16] Nor did Microsoft view as an immediate threat the possibility that a new technology would leapfrog its current and planned operating system technologies.[17]

Microsoft argued that it faced competition from its own installed base. But because of the absence of other competition, it does not follow that whatever constraint its own installed base posed was sufficient to prevent Microsoft from having monopoly power; indeed, the contrary is the case. New operating systems are principally acquired in connection with the purchase of new computers and only secondarily in connection with upgrades. At best, Microsoft's installed-base argument relates to its pricing of upgrades. The argument does not apply to the more important channel of new computers, which are bought largely to take advantage of developments in hardware or software. The fact that a given user has an old operating system will not do much to keep that user from changing computers when hardware or software improves and a new computer is required to use those improvements.

Moreover, Microsoft took actions to ensure that installed-base competition was minimal. Microsoft's licenses preclude customers from transferring their licenses to other PCs. That both limits installed-base competition as new PCs are bought and prevents the development of a secondary market in licenses that would permit original equipment manufacturers to acquire them as an alternative to licensing the use of Microsoft's newest version of its operating system. Microsoft's contracts with original equipment manufacturers also generally prohibited them from shipping PCs to consumers with earlier versions of Microsoft's operating system once a new version is released.

Despite all the evidence set out above, Microsoft denied that it has monopoly power. In the firm's defense Richard Schmalensee used the standard static model for short-run monopoly pricing as one basis for his conclusion that Microsoft lacks such power. In his analysis he assumed that monopoly power existed, estimated the elasticity of demand for Windows by starting with the elasticity of demand for PCs and the fact that PCs and Windows are typically sold together, took the marginal cost of Windows as approximately zero, applied the formula, and derived the short-run monopoly price for Windows. Finding that the result was in excess of the actual price (around $60) by some $1,800, he concluded that the assumption of monopoly power must be in error.

We do not agree with that analysis. Apart from the fact that the calculations contained a number of material errors, the entire train of logic is not correct. Since Microsoft's marginal cost is essentially zero, the short-run profit-maximizing action for the firm is to price at the point where the elasticity of demand that it faces is unity. *That is true whether or not Microsoft has monopoly power.*

It is not credible—and is inconsistent with the evidence—to suppose that such is the case at a price around $60, since that would imply a loss of 10 percent of Windows sales if the price were increased by $6. Yet, substantial evidence was presented at trial that original equipment manufacturers would not shift to another operating system, even if the price of Windows rose significantly. Further, it is implausible that the original equipment manufacturers' own sales would drop by a significant amount. The correct conclusion must surely be that something other than short-run profit maximization is happening. Microsoft is simply taking its profits in other ways.

Effectively, Professor Schmalensee's logic is that monopoly power plus short-run profit maximization imply a price higher than observed. He concludes that no monopoly power exists. But—even apart from the errors in the calculation—the correct conclusion is that Microsoft is not maximizing its short-run profits.

We believe that Microsoft's pricing of its operating system—in particular, its contractual prices to original equipment manufacturers—is consistent with profit maximization by a firm with monopoly power.[18] It is possible, indeed likely, that Microsoft is not maximizing its short-run profits in its operating system pricing. In a network industry, it is in any dominant firm's interest to account in its pricing strategy for a host of factors that could lead, other things equal, to a lower price than one would expect. Those factors, which are not fully reflected in Professor Schmalensee's analysis, include: (1) the value of keeping and growing one's installed base, the source of the significant network effects; (2) the possibility of creating increased demand for complementary applications, which in turn provides an additional revenue source; (3) the need to discourage software pirating; and (4) the imposition of onerous restrictions on Microsoft's original equipment manufacturer customers as part of its anticompetitive campaign, discussed below, to preserve its long-run monopoly profits.

The Netscape Browser's Threat to Microsoft's Operating System Monopoly.

Eroding the applications programming barrier to entry. Microsoft recognized that the dominant position of its Windows operating system could be threatened by an Internet browser that was capable of supporting applications independent of the operating system.[19] To the extent that browsers themselves expose applications programming interfaces, they support applications independent of the operating system. Therefore, by lessening reliance on the operating system, the browser, while not performing all the traditional functions of an operating system, could have provided opportunities for competing operating systems by reducing the applications barrier to entry that protects Microsoft's operating system monopoly.

That threat was real because the Navigator browser runs on many different operating systems, including Windows, the Apple Macintosh operating system, and various flavors of UNIX. Netscape's browsers contain their own set of applications programming interfaces—as well as a set of Java applications programming interfaces—to which applications developers can write their applications. As a result, developers can create applications that will run on browsers regardless of the underlying operating system. It is important to note that the "natural" applications barrier to entry would not protect Microsoft from such a development. Unlike a rival operating system, Netscape's Navigator provided an application—a complement to the operating system. Since Internet browsing was becoming extremely popular, computer users would acquire Navigator to use that application. If that occurred, then it would become increasingly attractive for software developers to write to the Navigator applications programming interfaces, and computer users would care less and less about the underlying operating system.

Similarly, browsers could have reduced the power of the operating system monopoly by facilitating the expansion of network computing, in which users with "thin clients" use a network to access applications residing on a server computer, rather than host the application on the PC itself. Microsoft's own documents show a constant awareness of browsers as a serious threat to its operating system monopoly, and its executives expressed in both depositions and internal documents their concern that browsers would weaken Microsoft's control of the platform.[20]

Microsoft's plan to extend its control to the browser market. Microsoft responded to the Netscape threat by adopting a strategy aimed at extending its dominance over PC operating systems to Internet browsers. Microsoft recognized that it could protect its dominant position in the PC operating systems market by gaining and keeping a large share of the business in Internet browsers and by preventing any other browser from having a sufficient share to threaten Microsoft's platform dominance or to remain viable as a platform.[21] Moreover, if Microsoft's Internet Explorer browser (IE) were the dominant browser and Microsoft decided to support only Windows-based technology, developers would have little incentive to create applications that were not Windows-based.[22]

Microsoft took a number of anticompetitive actions to exclude competition in Internet browsers. They were acts that Microsoft would not have undertaken except to exclude and foreclose competition and protect the applications barrier to entry.

Microsoft's Attempts to Allocate Markets.

The June 1995 attempt to divide markets with Netscape. Microsoft's activities to prevent the emergence of the browser as a platform threat were part of a course of conduct that was undertaken to prevent other firms from developing platform software that might threaten the Windows operating system monopoly.

One of the first actions Microsoft took to stem the incipient threat that browsers posed to its monopoly was, in 1995, to solicit its emerging competitor, Netscape, to engage in a market allocation scheme. Microsoft's attempt to enter into a horizontal agreement with Netscape to eliminate Netscape as a competitor supplying browsers for Windows 95 is significant because, if Netscape had agreed, Microsoft would have succeeded in eliminating its only serious browser competitor. The attempt is also significant because it helps reveal the purpose of actions taken by Microsoft when Netscape refused to agree to divide markets.[23] Since Windows was the most popular operating system by far, an agreement by Netscape not to produce a browser for Windows would have eliminated Navigator as a threat to the applications barrier to entry.

Similar conduct with Intel and Apple. Microsoft also engaged in similar conduct with Intel and Apple. When Intel proposed offering certain platform-level software that conflicted with Microsoft's platform plans, Microsoft threatened, among other things, to withhold support for new generations of Intel processors if Intel proceeded with its plans. In the words of Intel chairman Andrew S. Grove, Intel ultimately "caved" and withdrew the effort, at least under its own brand. He explained, "Introducing a Windows-based software initiative that Microsoft doesn't support . . . well, life is too short for that."[24]

Microsoft's internal documents, including particularly confidential messages from Bill Gates personally, confirm Microsoft's attempt to convince Intel to agree not to engage in platform competition with Microsoft by developing its Native Signal Processing (NSP) technology, which would have endowed microprocessors with enhanced video and audio capabilities.[25] Because the NSP technology would have been available for non-Windows platforms, it could have presented a threat to Microsoft's monopoly power.[26]

Steven McGeady of Intel explained that Microsoft also discouraged Intel from supporting Netscape or Java as an alternative platform.[27] Similarly, Microsoft documents confirm that Microsoft used its relationship with Intel to discourage Intel from supporting Java or Netscape's browser.[28] The documents show that Microsoft engaged in extensive efforts to convince Intel not to support competing technologies, even when those competing technologies would enhance the performance of Windows PCs.[29]

Microsoft also attempted to suppress platform-level competition from Apple. Timothy Schaaff described how Apple promoted QuickTime, its multimedia streaming technology, as an audio-visual content creation/authoring and playback mechanism on the Windows operating systems.[30] Microsoft, however, considered audio-visual streaming technologies to be part of a "growing collection of technologies" that "were a threat to the Windows platform." Beginning in 1997, Microsoft representatives informed Apple that "Microsoft wanted to have control over the user interface . . . and that Microsoft was determined that the essential applications programming interfaces that were the foundation of the operating system should all come from Microsoft and not come from a third party."[31] Microsoft offered to forgo competing in the multimedia authoring tools market if Apple would scale back its efforts to establish QuickTime as a multimedia platform on the Windows operating system. In addition to that inducement, Microsoft also set forth a threat: in the absence of an accommodation, Microsoft could devote 100 to 150 engineers to competing against Apple in the authoring tools market even though, as Microsoft's representative put it, such action made "no sense from a business standpoint."[32]

As those incidents indicate, Microsoft was prepared to respond immediately to prevent the long-run threat of any other firm from writing platform-level software.[33] That was true even though, in the short run, the software could increase the functionality and performance of, and thus the demand for, Windows-based PCs.

Microsoft's conduct with respect to Intel and Apple is consistent with its efforts to prevent browsers from becoming a threat to the applications barrier to entry. In each case, Microsoft was confronted with platform-level software to which applications programs could be written. In each case, platform-level applications programming interfaces threatened to erode the applications barrier to entry into PC operating systems by supporting applications programs that could be used with multiple operating systems. In each case, Microsoft responded by attempting to get the supplier of the potential alternative platform-level software to agree to withdraw from offering it and to concentrate instead on products that did not offer platform potential. In each case, Microsoft was prepared to act to preclude the supplier of a potential platform-level software from succeeding in offering the platform, even if such actions did not "make sense from a business standpoint."

Predatory campaign to exclude browser competition. Microsoft's response to the prospect of a successful Netscape browser with cross-platform applications programming interfaces that could erode the applications barrier to entry was to engage in predatory conduct. Once Microsoft recognized the potential threat posed by Netscape's browser, Microsoft began devoting at least $100 million per year to developing its own browser. Microsoft also spent tens of millions of dollars a year marketing and promoting IE.[34]

Despite the significant browser-related costs it was incurring, Microsoft distributed its browser at a negative price. The IE browser was not only given away free; companies were also paid money and given valuable concessions to accept, use, distribute, and promote IE.[35] Microsoft's internal documents make clear that Microsoft undertook its browser development not to make money from browsers, but to prevent Netscape's browser from facilitating competition with Microsoft's monopoly operating system.

One Microsoft document, while hardly unique, is especially revealing. Under the heading "Own Corporate Browser Licensing," Brad Chase of Microsoft wrote: "This is one of the biggest potential revenue opportunities for Netscape.... [W]e should have absolute dominant browser share in the corporate space. . . . [M]ake it very clear it does not make sense for them to buy Netscape Navigator."[36]

Interestingly, Microsoft undertook detailed studies of Netscape's sources of revenue and what Netscape required to survive as an effective competitor. When Microsoft made its decision to supply IE without charge, the firm estimated that from 20 percent to 50 percent of Netscape's revenues came from licensing its browser.[37] Microsoft thus decided to price its own browser below cost when it knew that Netscape was charging for its browser and that Netscape depended on those revenues to continue to compete effectively. Indeed, Microsoft candidly described its pricing of its browser to Intel in an effort to convince Intel not to do business with Netscape; Microsoft said that it was "going to be distributing the browser for free" and that "this strategy would cut off Netscape's air supply, keep them from gaining any revenue to reinvest in their business."[38]

Without the gain to Microsoft that would result from preserving its highly profitable operating system monopoly and from monopolizing the browser market, the firm's conduct does not make good business sense. Microsoft was giving away something that it had spent a lot of money to develop and distribute and something for which the leading competitor was charging. It is only when Microsoft's gains from preserving and extending its monopoly are included that its conduct appears to be profitable.

At trial, Microsoft argued that its conduct was profitable without considering gains from reducing competition because wide distribution of its browser causes more people to buy PCs to browse the Internet, with the result that Microsoft sells more copies of its Windows operating system. That argument is incorrect, in part for the following reasons. First, Microsoft's internal documents do not support the suggestion that either the purpose or effect of Microsoft's predatory pricing of browsers was to increase sales of Windows. Second, as an analytical matter, browsers can be complements to operating systems to the extent that the sale of browsers that can be used with Windows will increase demand for Windows. But whatever Microsoft's interest in developing its own browser, it should have no interest in taking from users (and their proxies, original equipment manufacturers), in whole or in part, the option to choose the complements that maximize the value of the operating system for them. But Microsoft cared greatly who made the browsers used with Windows. Indeed, Microsoft tried to discourage Netscape from offering Netscape's browser for use with Windows—an action inconsistent with Microsoft's efforts to take browser sales away from others. Third, Microsoft devoted substantial time, effort, and money to developing and distributing a version of IE for Apple computers. Microsoft gets no money from increasing sales of Apple's operating system; indeed, since Apple offers the main alternative to a PC using Windows, promoting complements to Apple that increase Apple's attractiveness to users *reduces* sales of Windows.[39] Fourth, Microsoft was preoccupied not with increasing total sales of browsers, but with its *share* of browser sales. Indeed, Microsoft studied and tried to implement ways to disable Netscape and reduce total browser sales. Such conduct does not make business sense if browsers are viewed as a means of increasing sales of Windows. But that conduct is sensible if browsers are viewed as a competitive threat to Microsoft's Windows monopoly.

Microsoft also argued that it undertook its actions to earn ancillary revenues from IE, largely from gaining a portal Internet site and accompanying ancillary revenues. That argument is incorrect. No evidence exists that Microsoft *ever* considered such revenues until after the trial had begun. Indeed, Microsoft referred to IE as a "no-revenue product."[40] In addition, Microsoft concluded that Netscape could not be profitable simply from such portal revenues while it was forced to give away its browser. Moreover, as described below, Microsoft took actions that it knew would "put a bullet in the head" of its own Internet service, MSN (Microsoft Network), to encourage America Online (AOL) to adopt IE.[41]

Furthermore, Microsoft's contracts with Internet service providers penalized them for excessive distribution of Netscape, even if they also distributed IE. Most revealing of all, Microsoft permitted original equipment manufacturers to put their own "shells" on a browser and thus to direct users to their own portal sites *provided that the browser was IE*. That suggests that Microsoft was concerned only about the technology—the applications programming interfaces that the browser would expose to software developers—and not about the portal revenues.

We note that *Microsoft* does not relate to a situation where a product is sold at a price that arguably covers some definition of cost; in the present case, Microsoft distributed its browser at a zero (indeed, a negative)[42] price. Furthermore, *Microsoft* is not a situation in which there is doubt as to the purpose of a company's pricing; in the present case, Microsoft made clear that the purpose of its decision to distribute its browser for free was to "cut off Netscape's air supply." Moreover, this case is not a situation in which any doubt exists as to a company's ability to recoup forgone profits through the preservation or obtaining of monopoly power. The preservation of Microsoft's operating system monopoly alone would permit recoupment. Finally, *Microsoft* is not a case in which a company sets a price below cost with the reasonable expectation that such pricing will result in competitive revenues from other products or services; Microsoft's contemporaneous documents show no sign that the company's zero (or negative) price for its browser was considered a way to earn competitive ancillary revenues. Rather, that price was considered a way to prevent potential competition from alternative platforms.[43]

Microsoft's predatory pricing was part of, and should be evaluated in connection with, its broader campaign to eliminate Netscape's Navigator and Sun's Java as sources of potential danger to the applications barrier to entry protecting Microsoft's operating system monopoly. That was a campaign characterized by actions in which Microsoft lost money to raise rivals' costs and exclude them from the market;[44] by actions that Microsoft recognized internally did not "make sense from a business standpoint," except for their anticompetitive effects; and by Microsoft's agreements with customers and competitors that required them to refuse to deal with Netscape—or to do so only on unfavorable terms.

Microsoft's determination to restrict the support and distribution of Netscape's browser by Apple is particularly significant when one considers that Apple represents the main potential alternative to desktop PCs running Microsoft's Windows. Whatever the relevance of Microsoft's arguments about why it wanted to make IE available to sell more copies of Windows, those arguments cannot apply to Microsoft's efforts to force Apple to distribute IE. In addition, no legitimate justification exists for Microsoft and

Apple—two competitors—to enter into an agreement "to undermine SUN."[45]

Microsoft's Bundling of Its Browser with Its Monopoly Operating System and Its Restrictions on Original Equipment Manufacturers.

Decision to bundle IE with Windows. Although IE was not originally "tied" or "bundled" with the retail version of Windows 95 when it was first released in the summer of 1995, Microsoft did bundle IE with Windows 95 in distributing Windows 95 to original equipment manufacturers, and IE is now bundled with all Windows 95 and Windows 98 operating systems that Microsoft distributes through retail or original equipment manufacturer channels.[46] In Windows 98 the browser has been designed to share extensive code with the operating system. Microsoft made the decision to bundle IE and Windows in one form or another even though there is demand for browsers separate from the demand for operating systems.[47]

Microsoft made its bundling decision not to achieve efficiencies, but to foreclose competition.[48] The problem is not that Microsoft offered original equipment manufacturers and users a bundled version of Windows and IE; it is that Microsoft did not give them the option of taking Windows without the browser. The firm thus compelled those original equipment manufacturers and users that wished otherwise to take IE to get Windows. That foreclosure of competition had an immediate harmful effect on consumers, whose choice of browsers was restricted and who faced substantial uncertainty.[49] The harm was not simply to consumers who faced limited browser choice; other harms resulted from the unnecessarily cumbersome operating system and from the limited options of those who preferred not to use a browser.[50]

Microsoft also recognized that original equipment manufacturers wanted the ability to develop their own screens and substitute Netscape's browser for IE. As a result, in 1996 Microsoft imposed screen and start-up restrictions to prevent original equipment manufacturers from developing their own first screen or positioning competing browsers more favorably than IE. Presumably, the original equipment manufacturers wished to do other things as a way of attracting and serving their customers. Indeed, original equipment manufacturers can be expected to make a profit-maximizing choice of browser to sell with their operating system products. To the extent that Microsoft cares that the browsers used with its Windows products are high quality, it can rest assured that the original equipment manufacturers' incentives are aligned with its own.

Restrictive agreements with PC manufacturers. In connection with its tying of IE and Windows, Microsoft required the distribution of IE and restricted the distribution of other browsers by entering into restrictive agreements with PC original equipment manufacturers. The agreements required original equipment manufacturers who wanted to preinstall Windows 95 or Windows 98 on their machines—meaning all PC manufacturers—also to preinstall Microsoft's IE. The agreements also limited the ability of original equipment manufacturers to promote other browsers or to substitute other browsers for IE. Indeed, until an early 1998 stipulation between Microsoft and the Department of Justice prompted changes, the agreements typically required that licensees not modify or delete any of the product software. That prevented original equipment manufacturers from removing any part of IE from the operating system, including the visible means of user access to the IE software, such as the IE icon on the Windows desktop or the IE entry in the "start" menu.

Licensees were not contractually restricted from loading other browsers on the desktop. But some original equipment manufacturers preferred to load only one browser to avoid user confusion and the resulting consumer support costs and to avoid increased testing costs.[51] In addition, some original equipment manufacturers viewed the desktop and disk space as scarce real estate and were generally reluctant to preinstall more than one software title in each functional category.[52]

Microsoft modified restrictions on the start-up screen just before trial, so that original equipment manufacturers had somewhat more flexibility than when the restrictions were imposed. But IE must still be installed on every PC, and the IE icon cannot be removed. The result is a significant exclusionary effect that ensures that IE is the *only* browser on most PCs shipped by original equipment manufacturers.[53] By January 1999, Navigator was on the desktop of only a very small percentage of the PCs being shipped.[54]

Agreement with Apple. Microsoft also entered into a restrictive agreement with Apple that required Apple to make IE its default browser on all its Macintosh operating systems. That agreement forced Apple to place all competing browsers in a folder, thereby removing other browsers from the Macintosh desktop, and limited Apple's ability to promote other browsers.[55] To induce Apple to enter that contract, Microsoft, among other things, threatened to stop development of its Office application suite for the Macintosh. As Microsoft knew, withdrawal of support for that crucial application would have had a devastating effect on the viability of the Macintosh operating system.[56] Since Microsoft derives revenue from licensing that application to Macintosh users (and none from IE), carrying out the threat, or even making it, could not have been profit-maximizing except for the effects on the browser wars and the applications barrier to entry.

Justifications for bundling and restrictions on original equipment manufacturers. Microsoft proffered a number of justifications for its conduct, but none suggests that the firm's primary motive was anything other than to restrict competition in browsers.

Microsoft designed interdependencies between IE and Windows 98 and claimed that this was the rationale for its bundling practices. But even if two products as designed cannot readily be separated, the bundling or tying of the two can raise the same anticompetitive concerns that contractual bundling or tying would raise. Moreover, such concerns are not automatically overcome merely because the bundle brings some amount of consumer benefit to certain consumers.

Virtually every product design, particularly in the area of computer software, can make a plausible claim for some efficiency or benefit. Many software products can be combined in such a way that they share certain code; if code is shared, there is some plausible efficiency—although perhaps very slight—and separating the two products once they have been combined may be very difficult. If combining two products in a way that produces plausible efficiencies— however slight—or that makes it difficult to separate the products were an absolute defense to a claim that the combination was anticompetitive, software commerce would be essentially immune from tying scrutiny. In the present case, the evidence clearly shows that the anticompetitive effects are large, whereas the technological benefits appear to be small or nonexistent.

Microsoft's chief technology officer, James Allchin, testified that the same consumer experience given by Windows 98, where the browser is welded into the operating system, was provided by Windows 95 and IE 4. Recall that IE is effectively added on top of a browserless operating system. No benefits obtainable by putting separate IE and operating system code together exist that cannot be obtained otherwise.[57] Indeed, Edward W. Felten, assistant professor of computer science at Princeton University, testifying for the government, pointed out that Windows 95 need not have been so designed. That testimony supports the view that boxing IE and Windows code together produces no benefits that one cannot get otherwise.[58] Therefore, Microsoft's pressure on Apple to use IE cannot have been driven by any such technological explanation.

In the context of an earlier proceeding involving a Microsoft consent decree, the Court of Appeals for the District of Columbia Circuit suggested *in dicta* that an innovation bringing any consumer benefit, no matter how small, would prevent analysis of anticompetitive effects, no matter how large.[59] We are concerned that if such a doctrine were to be extended to antitrust law generally, it would provide an open invitation for firms to cloak exclusionary acts in minor innovations. Microsoft's argument that no distinction then existed between the operating system and the browser brings that issue to the forefront.

Microsoft argued that it must force original equipment manufacturers to take IE because the absence of IE might undermine the quality of the operating system, to the detriment of users. But several facts contradict that suggestion. For example, Microsoft provided ways to remove IE in Windows 95—a function that would most likely not have been provided if it decreased the quality of the operating system. Also, we have seen compelling evidence that it is possible within Windows 98 to remove the ability to browse the Web with IE and to replace IE with another browser with no appreciable decline in the quality of the Windows 98 operating system.[60]

In fact, Microsoft permitted Dell to remove IE from the desktop for Windows 95 at the request of that original equipment manufacturer's large customers. Presumably, Microsoft would not allow that kind of exception if it undermined the quality of the operating system. Likewise, original equipment manufacturers would not negotiate to remove IE if the operating system would be adversely affected, since a poorly operating computer would reflect unfavorably on the original equipment manufacturer and would be likely to increase the number of customer support calls. Also, large customers would not request an operating system with IE removed if they thought that doing so would adversely affect the system.

As noted above, Microsoft now allows original equipment manufacturers slightly more flexibility on the first screen and the Internet service provider registration process. It seems unlikely that either Microsoft or the original equipment manufacturers believe that those changes will lead to significant deterioration of the quality of the operating system.

Microsoft also argued that its bundling of IE is necessary to provide a uniform platform for software developers. We note, however, in light of the different versions of Windows and IE that Microsoft has put in the marketplace, that developers relying on system services or code found in IE must redistribute the necessary IE code anyway to ensure that the proper version of the necessary dynamic link library or file is present to support their applications.[61]

Microsoft argued that it is justified in restricting original equipment manufacturers from altering the start-up process to preserve the quality and speed of the start-up process and to give each user a consistent experience. But the fact that Microsoft has granted exceptions to those restrictions for certain original equipment manufacturers suggests that the concern for quality, speed, and consistency is not Microsoft's primary motive for enforcing those restrictions.

If Microsoft did not have monopoly power, it would not have an incentive to engage in anticompetitive—that is, otherwise unprofitable—bundling, because it would not have the market power to force unwanted code on users and, except in the case where a substantial increase in market power was a likely result, it would not have monopoly returns sufficient to justify an otherwise unprofitable bundling strategy. Absent monopoly power, bundling is likely to be harmless and to serve legitimate business purposes, because bundling is not a rational anticompetitive strategy for a firm that lacks significant market power. We conclude that those types of provisions are anticompetitive. They inhibit PC manufacturers from preinstalling and promoting competing browsers. Their purpose and effect is to weaken browser competition to protect Microsoft's business in operating systems. The benefit gained by creating interdependencies between IE and Windows would have to be great to counterbalance the anticompetitive effects of bundling.

Exclusionary Agreements with Internet Service Providers. Microsoft also required the promotion and distribution of IE—and restricted the promotion and distribution of other browsers—by striking deals with Internet service providers to protect Microsoft's business in operating systems. Internet service providers and the online services are, after original equipment manufacturers, the largest distributors of browsers.

Because of the monopoly position of Microsoft's Windows operating system, Internet service providers are very interested in having favorable placement on the Windows desktop to attract subscribers. Microsoft understood that and, as part of its effort to exploit its Windows advantage, designed a special access method called the Internet Connection Wizard to assist users in signing up for Internet service providers. Only a few Internet service providers could be accessed through the Internet Connection Wizard. Initially, there were twelve, including some of the largest Internet service providers.

By mid-August of 1996, Microsoft had signed "IE Preferred" distribution agreements with about 2,500 Internet service providers, including most of the largest in the United States. Those agreements usually specified that IE would be the preferred and default browser. While the Internet service providers could distribute other browsers, Microsoft's contracts with Internet service providers who received a preferred placement on the desktop typically required that the Internet service providers not distribute other browsers to more than a relatively small fraction of their customers.

Microsoft also created another desktop folder for Internet service providers that were online services providers and entered into agreements with AOL, CompuServe, Prodigy, and AT&T to appear in it.

Microsoft used the strong demand by online services for access to Microsoft's Windows operating system to extract promises from the services not to deal with Netscape or to do so only on very unfavorable terms.[62] In particular, Microsoft reached an agreement with AOL, which by early 1996 was being installed on a large number of PCs, to ship IE.

While Microsoft charged a referral fee for customers the Internet service providers acquired through the Windows 95 desktop, browser share, not revenue, was the object of the agreements. Microsoft also made valuable concessions, directly or indirectly, to the Internet service providers. The concessions varied across those providers but included joint marketing programs, pricing deals, and discounts on referral fees for users switched from competitive browsers.

In particular, Microsoft offered AOL a substantial discount in referral fees if it would ship IE. Microsoft explicitly recognized that the decision to grant online services—particularly AOL—favorable access to Windows was an expensive one.[63]

In return, Microsoft extracted strong restrictions on Netscape. Those were not, as Microsoft claimed, merely joint marketing agreements. For one thing, the product being "jointly marketed"—IE—was in Microsoft's own words "a no-revenue product." In addition, the Internet service providers had to accept restrictions on their shipment of other browsers not just to subscribers acquired through placement in Windows, but to *all* subscribers, however acquired.

Little doubt exists that AOL's performance under the restrictive agreement with Microsoft had strong positive effects on Microsoft's browser share. Importantly, Microsoft did not waive restrictions on AOL and the other online services in 1998 when, on the eve of the litigation, Microsoft modified restrictions for many other Internet service providers.

As this chapter was being written, AOL continued to ship IE despite its late 1998 acquisition of Netscape. AOL has renewed its arrangement with Microsoft through 2001 and affirmed its intention to continue. This is what economic analysis leads us to expect. If, without the merger, the benefits to AOL of using IE exceeded the sum of the benefits to AOL from using Netscape and the benefits to Netscape of being used by AOL, then, unless the merger increased the latter sum, the decision by the merged entity should remain the same. Moreover, while a decision by AOL to switch to Navigator might threaten the applications barrier to entry, such a threat is not necessarily more plausible after the merger than before, particularly since Microsoft's actions averted the browser danger to the barrier. Even were that not the case, the value to AOL of facilitating a challenge to Microsoft's monopoly power in operating systems must be far less than the value to Microsoft of preventing that challenge. Hence, at most, the AOL acquisition of Netscape may increase the rents that Microsoft has to pay to AOL to preserve the barrier. It will not affect the barrier itself.

While some variation existed in the restrictions imposed on the online services and other Internet service providers, those agreements with Microsoft limited the Internet service providers' ability to promote and distribute third-party browsers. In general, the agreements stated that Microsoft would provide users with access to Internet service providers from the desktop, and in return, those providers were required not only to promote IE, but not to promote other browsers. Typically, such restrictive provisions involved percentage restrictions on shipping for larger Internet service providers and restrictions on promotional efforts for smaller Internet service providers.

Those limitations included requirements that 75 percent or more of the Internet service provider software shipments include IE as the only browser and that the Internet service provider not ship a competing browser unless a customer specifically requested it. In addition, the agreements placed limitations on Internet service provider links to use or download third-party browsers on the Internet service provider home Web page or any other Internet access service Web page offered by the Internet service provider. The agreements also placed limitations on the *total* shipments of non-Microsoft browsers by Internet service providers.[64] The limitations applied to shipments to *all* subscribers, not just to those obtained through favorable placement in the Windows desktop. The agreements also imposed prohibitions on expressing or implying that an alternative browser is available, including limitations on displaying any logo for a non-IE Web browser on the Internet service provider home Web page or any other Internet access service Web page offered by the Internet service provider.

By early 1998, Microsoft had become aware that it was on the verge of being sued by the Department of Justice. It is not surprising therefore that, in April of 1998, Microsoft issued a statement to certain Internet service providers with whom it had restrictive agreements that waived some of the restrictions in their agreements. For example, in a letter to Earthlink, Microsoft committed not to enforce provisions concerning distribution volumes or percentages, discussion, promotion, or advertising of IE and the use of IE as a standard or default browser. In addition, Microsoft removed restrictions, performance obligations, and qualifications for referral fees.[65]

Nevertheless, Internet service providers included in the Internet Connection Wizard were—and are—still prohibited from distributing and promoting Navigator with "preference." IE must be discussed, promoted, or advertised so that, in its entirety, its treatment is no less prominent and favorable than that accorded to Navigator. Even as regards other Internet service providers, Microsoft remains free to reimpose even the waived restrictions, and, whatever the extent of Microsoft's waiver, it did not undo the harm to competition that had already occurred.

In its agreements, Microsoft offered Internet service providers valuable space on its desktop as well as direct payments in the form of rebates or bounties. In exchange, Microsoft placed requirements on Internet service providers that hindered their ability to promote or distribute Netscape Navigator. Again, given Microsoft's position in operating systems, those provisions were anticompetitive. Their purpose and effect were to reduce the ability of competing browser manufacturers to distribute and promote their browsers through leading Internet service providers. Regardless of whether such provisions would in themselves be anticompetitive if put in place by a company with a small share of operating systems, they are certainly anticompetitive when Microsoft uses them to protect its dominant position in operating systems.

Exclusionary Agreements with Internet Content Providers. Microsoft also had restrictive agreements with Internet content providers. At the time of those agreements, Microsoft promoted the use of IE and restricted the promotion and distribution of other browsers in its agreements with Internet content providers for its desktop Channel Bar. Internet content providers valued the opportunity to have a channel on the Microsoft desktop, because it encouraged users to visit the Internet content providers' Web sites, which in turn increased the Internet content providers' ability to promote their own products and to sell advertising space on their Web pages.

Although the Channel Bar was not a success, it is still worth mentioning one provision of some of the agreements because it is a clear guide to Microsoft's purposes. While Microsoft permitted Internet content providers to appear on another browser's—read "Netscape's"—site, it forbade them to pay the other browser company for such appearance or for promoting the Internet content provider. That provision can have no proper procompetitive purpose. Its only purpose was to cut Netscape's revenue and thus to hamper further Netscape's ability to compete with IE.

Limiting the Availability and Success of Cross-Platform Java Technology. As discussed previously, Microsoft recognized Sun Microsystems' Java as a threat to its operating system monopoly because Java, like browsers, offered the potential for eroding the applications barrier to entry. Microsoft's anticompetitive actions restrained the use and availability of Java technology to protect the current dominance of the Windows operating system.

A Java Runtime Environment, which consists of a Java Virtual Machine, the Java platform core classes, and supporting files, is a software layer with its own applications programming interface set that resides on top of an operating system and is designed to allow applications written in Java to function on different operating systems. Significantly, browsers—that is, non-Microsoft browsers—are an important distribution channel for Java Runtime Environments.

Microsoft undertook two basic approaches to eliminating the potential competitive threat posed by Java. First, Microsoft, recognizing that Netscape's browser was the primary distribution method for Java, sought to eliminate Java by eliminating Netscape's browser as a viable alternative.[66] Second, Microsoft took actions to impede the cross-platform potential of Java by developing an interface called J/Direct. Any application that uses "J/Direct will run only on the Microsoft virtual machine."

Microsoft did not seek to "kill cross-platform Java" merely by developing its own version of Java and marketing it on the merits. Instead, Microsoft sought to "kill cross-platform Java" by developing what it termed "polluted Java."[67] It did so in two principal ways. First, the default way of writing applications and "applets" (small applications) for Microsoft's virtual machine causes some of those applications and applets not to be able to run properly on non-Windows platforms, or even on non-Microsoft virtual machines running on Windows.[68] Second, if application developers used the software developer tools that Microsoft provided for Java, then—without intending to do so—they would wind up with an application that effectively would not run on non-Windows platforms. Those were not the profit-maximizing actions of a company competing on the merits. Together with Microsoft's actions against browsers, they were acts specifically directed at preserving Microsoft's monopoly power in operating systems.

Anticompetitive Effects. Microsoft's conduct prevented its browser competitors, principally Netscape, from effectively competing on the merits for new business, artificially raised barriers to entry into both the browser and the operating system markets, and preserved Microsoft's operating system monopoly.

The significance of new installations. The vast majority of browser users tend to stay with the browser they receive with their PC if there is one or, if not, the browser provided by their Internet service provider.[69] By ensuring that virtually all new users receive Microsoft's browser either with their PC or from their Internet service provider or both, Microsoft effectively excluded Netscape and other browser competitors from the market and thus limited them to a declining base of existing users.

Foreclosing browser competitors from competing on the merits. Microsoft recognized that it would not be able to compete successfully against Netscape on the merits of IE alone, in part because, while no company is perfect, and while Netscape—like Microsoft—made mistakes, Microsoft recognized the strengths of Netscape's product offerings.[70] Microsoft's response was to exclude Netscape and other browser competitors from the two most important channels of distribution—original equipment manufacturers and Internet service providers. Those channels are critical to browser distribution because many users get their browser from one or the other—and because few users switch from one browser to another unless they buy a new computer or switch Internet service providers. Microsoft succeeded in effectively excluding Netscape almost completely from the personal computer original equipment manufacturer distribution channel. Original equipment manufacturers that license Windows were required to take—and not remove—IE, and for most original equipment manufacturers, including the largest, that means including only IE with the PCs they ship.

Another important browser distribution channel is through Internet service providers, including online services. There, Microsoft's restrictive agreements with AOL and CompuServe alone tied up Internet service providers/online services with 65 percent of the subscribers to Internet service providers/online services considered to be in the "top 80" by Microsoft at year-end 1997.[71] Indeed, more than 95 percent of subscribers to Internet service providers in the "top 80" subscribe to Internet service providers that were contractually required to distribute IE preferentially.[72]

Microsoft asserted that its anticompetitive practices do not result in foreclosure because users can download browsers for free from the Internet. It is important to remember, though, that users prefer to get their browsers installed on their computers because consumers pay in terms of time and trouble to download a browser from the Internet. Indeed, Microsoft's own studies show that most Internet users have never downloaded a browser.[73] What is important is not whether users can download a competitor's browser, but whether users *will* download a competitor's browser under prevailing market conditions.

Microsoft claimed that competitors can distribute browsers effectively and that Netscape had distributed or would have distributed by its partners 250 million to 270 million copies of its browser in 1997 and 1998. Netscape did not, however, intend to do any of that distribution, and Netscape's distribution by CD-ROM was "almost none."[74] Further, to the extent that the distribution is to be by mail, it is a very inefficient distribution method. Because it takes time and trouble to install software, customers are unlikely to switch to another browser if they already have a browser that is up and running. Relegating Netscape to distributing its software by mail is simply a means of raising rivals' costs.

We can see the evidence of Microsoft's foreclosure of Netscape and other browser competitors by comparing Microsoft's share of browsers distributed by Internet service providers that have made IE their default browser with Internet service providers that have not done so.[75] At the end of 1997, Microsoft enjoyed a 94 percent weighted average share of browser shipments made by Internet service providers agreeing to make IE their default browser, compared with a 14 percent weighted average share of browser shipments by Internet service providers that did not make IE their default browser. Further, Microsoft's weighted average share of browser usage by subscribers to Internet service providers using IE as their default browser was over 60 percent. In contrast, Microsoft's weighted average share of the browser usage of subscribers to Internet service providers that did not make IE their default was less than 20 percent.

We can also analyze the difference in IE usage across subscribers of different Internet service providers by looking at IE's share of "hits" as reported by AdKnowledge, Inc., a company that develops and markets advertisement management products for the World Wide Web. We obtained a sample of AdKnowledge data to analyze how Microsoft's share of the browser market varies across Internet service providers, some of which have entered into agreements to distribute IE preferentially, and some of which have not entered into such agreements. While the AdKnowledge data are not so complete as one might wish,[76] they show trends that are unmistakable.

Figure 1-1, government exhibit 4, shows Microsoft's monthly share of browser usage by three categories of Internet service providers from January 1997 through August 1998. The top line shows Microsoft's share of usage among subscribers to AOL and CompuServe rising sharply. Those companies—now merged—were chosen because they represent the largest Internet service providers—with a total of more than 11.5 million subscribers and about 65 percent of all subscribers to the services in the "top 80" as of year-end 1997—and because AOL and CompuServe, as online service providers, were contractually restricted in their promotion and distribution of non-IE browsers to a greater extent than were most other Internet service providers. The middle line shows Microsoft's share for all Internet service providers. The bottom line shows Microsoft's share for the Internet service providers within the "top 80" that Microsoft listed as having "IE parity"— Internet service providers whose browser choice was not known to be contractually restricted—that had 10,000 or more subscribers, and for which data were available.

The effects are striking. Microsoft's share of "IE parity" browser usage—the category that is contractually neutral—rises in twenty months from 20 percent to just under 30 percent. That rise includes the effects of technological improvement in IE as well as the effects of Microsoft's bundling and tying. By contrast, the "all Internet service providers" line shows an increase in Microsoft's share from 20 percent to 49 percent. Finally, for AOL and CompuServe, Microsoft's share rose from just over 20 percent to over 87 percent. It is worth noting that the

FIGURE 1-1

MICROSOFT'S SHARE OF THE BROWSER MARKET:
MONTHLY USAGE BY INTERNET SERVICE PROVIDER CATEGORY

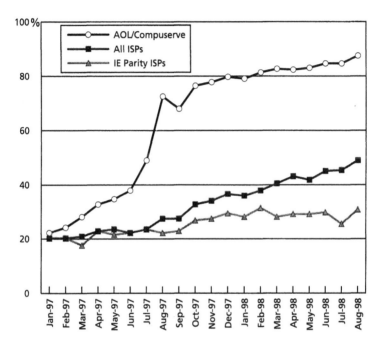

NOTE: This is Plaintiff's Exhibit 1092, MS98 0112834–36, and Government Exhibit 4.

SOURCE: AdKnowledge, Inc.

dramatic jump in that share occurred *before* the introduction of IE4 in October 1997.

The exclusion of Netscape and other browser competitors from the original equipment manufacturer channel has been even greater. Although several original equipment manufacturers—including the largest, Compaq—have sought to replace IE with Netscape, none is now permitted to do so. And the fact that IE inclusion is required means in most cases that only IE will be included.[77]

Microsoft's high and increasing browser market share. Because of Netscape's innovations and success in creating and distributing the world's first widely used browser, the firm initially had a very large share of the browser market. Microsoft's browser share at the beginning of calendar year 1997 was approximately 20 percent and had been significantly lower earlier.

Measuring precisely how the share has changed over time is difficult for several reasons. First, most share statistics are browser usage shares that reflect the usage of all browsers whenever acquired. Because of Netscape's large—and Microsoft's relatively small—share before 1997, present usage shares significantly understate Microsoft's share of current browser acquisitions. Second, usage shares are sometimes based on the number of browser users—in which case each browser used in the period measured is counted equally regardless of how often it is used in the period—and sometimes based on the number of times browsers are used in the period—in which case a browser is counted each time it is used. Regardless of how share is measured, however, Microsoft's browser share clearly increased dramatically, and Netscape's browser share fell sharply, over the years 1997 and 1998.[78] Indeed, Microsoft's browser share continued to increase through 1999 as well.

The AdKnowledge data show that Microsoft's share of incremental browser usage for the twenty months ending in August 1998 was 57 percent and that Netscape's incremental share of browser usage was 40 percent over the same period.[79] Since the incremental usage shares reflect increased usage of previously installed browsers, as well as the usage of browsers acquired during the period, even those incremental usage shares understate Microsoft's share—and overstate Netscape's share—of usage of new browsers.

Thus, substantial evidence exists that Microsoft's anticompetitive actions have permitted it to retain its power over price in operating systems and to inhibit development of Microsoft-independent innovations. Both acts harm consumer welfare.

Microsoft's anticompetitive actions are aimed at hindering the success of non-IE browsers but are likely to send a message to all software developers: Microsoft will impede any innovation that threatens Microsoft's monopoly in operating systems. That will lessen developers' incentives to create products that provide alternatives to the Windows platform. As a result, the range of software products consumers can choose from will be limited. Narrowed choice and slowed technological progress can never improve the welfare of consumers and are likely to decrease it. If Windows were truly a superior product, it would succeed on its merits. The actions Microsoft is taking will prevent that from being necessary.[80]

Concluding Comments

We believe that Microsoft engaged in a number of anticompetitive actions. In particular, taken together with Microsoft's other actions, the pricing of Microsoft's browser was anticompetitive; absent any expected deleterious effects on competition, the pricing would not be profit-maximizing. Moreover, Microsoft could recoup any forgone profits associated with its anticompetitive conduct through the protection of the firm's operating system monopoly.

If Microsoft's IE browser and Windows operating system are superior products, then competition will lead original equipment manufacturers, Internet service providers, Internet content providers, and customers to choose them, and Microsoft need not have artificially influenced those choices. But Microsoft has engaged in conduct that has no compelling economic justification but for its effect of restricting competition. Microsoft's actions have allowed it to protect its monopoly in the market for operating systems and to move toward establishing a monopoly in the market for browsers.[81]

Judge Jackson's findings of fact support the view that Microsoft's anticompetitive acts caused immediate harm. According to the court:

To the detriment of consumers . . . Microsoft has done much more than develop innovative browsing software of commendable quality and offer it bundled with Windows at no additional charge. . . . Microsoft also engaged in a concerted series of actions designed to protect the applications barrier to entry, and hence its monopoly power, from a variety of middleware threats, including Netscape's Web browser and Sun's implementation of Java.[82]

By refusing to offer those OEMs [original equipment manufacturers] who requested it a version of Windows without Web-browsing software, and by preventing OEMs from removing IE—or even the most obvious means of invoking it—prior to shipment, Microsoft forced OEMs to ignore consumer demand for a browserless version of Windows. . . . By ensuring that IE would launch in certain circumstances in Windows 98 even if Navigator were set as the default, and even if the consumer had removed all conspicuous means of invoking IE, Microsoft created confusion and frustration for consumers, and increased technical support costs for business customers. Those Windows purchasers who did not want browsing software . . . not only had to undertake the effort necessary to remove the visible means of invoking IE and then contend with the fact that IE would nevertheless launch in certain cases; they also had to . . . content themselves with a PC system that ran slower and provided less available memory than if the newest version of Windows came without browsing software. By constraining the freedom of OEMs to implement certain software programs in the Windows boot sequence, Microsoft foreclosed an opportunity for OEMs to make Windows PC systems less confusing and more user-friendly, as consumers desired. By taking the actions listed above, and by enticing firms into exclusivity arrangements with valuable inducements that only Microsoft could offer and that the firms reasonably believed they could not do without, Microsoft forced those consumers who otherwise would have elected Navigator as their browser to either pay a substantial price (in the forms of downloading, installation, confusion, degraded system performance, and diminished memory capacity) or content themselves with IE. Finally, by pressuring Intel to drop the development of platform-level NSP [native signal processing] software, and otherwise to cut back on its software development efforts, Microsoft deprived consumers of software innovation that they very well may have found valuable, had the innovation been allowed to reach the marketplace. None of these actions had pro-competitive justifications.[83]

Many of the tactics that Microsoft has employed have also harmed consumers indirectly by unjustifiably distorting competition. The actions that Microsoft took against Navigator hobbled a form of innovation that had shown the potential to depress the applications barrier to entry sufficiently to enable other firms to compete effectively against Microsoft in the market for Intel-compatible PC operating systems. That competition would have conduced to consumer choice and nurtured innovation. The campaign against Navigator also retarded widespread acceptance of Sun's Java implementation. . . . It is clear . . . that Microsoft has retarded, and perhaps altogether extinguished, the process by which . . . middleware technologies could have facilitated the introduction of competition into an important market.[84]

Most harmful of all is the message that Microsoft's actions have conveyed to every enterprise with the potential to innovate in the computer industry. Through its conduct toward Netscape, IBM, Compaq, Intel, and others, Microsoft has demonstrated that it will use its prodigious market power and immense profits to harm any firm that insists on pursuing initiatives that could intensify competition against one of Microsoft's core products. Microsoft's past success in hurting such companies and stifling innovation deters investment in technologies and businesses that exhibit the potential to threaten Microsoft. The ultimate result is that some innovations that would truly benefit consumers never occur for the sole reason that they do not coincide with Microsoft's self-interest.[85]

2

Be Nice to Your Rivals: How the Government Is Selling an Antitrust Case without Consumer Harm in *United States* v. *Microsoft*

David S. Evans and Richard L. Schmalensee

The modern rationale for antitrust is to protect consumers. But in *United States* v. *Microsoft*[1] the government could not show that Microsoft's actions had harmed consumers—or ever would.[2] Indeed, one need not go beyond the court's indictment of Microsoft near the end of its formal findings of fact to see that.[3] Instead of offering a compelling condemnation, the court concluded that Microsoft's actions "contributed to improving the quality of Web-browsing software, lowering its costs, and increasing its availability, thereby benefiting consumers" and that "[t]he debut of Internet Explorer and its rapid improvement gave Netscape an incentive to improve Navigator's quality at a competitive rate."[4] Moreover, the court conceded, "There is insufficient evidence to find that, absent Microsoft's actions, Navigator and Java already would have ignited genuine competition in the market for Intel-compatible PC operating systems."[5] To put it more succinctly, Microsoft's actions speeded innovation in

Web-browsing software and left consumers with the choice of two first-rate browsers instead of one.

So what has Microsoft done to warrant its unwilling participation in the antitrust show trial of the 1990s? The court notes that consumers who would have preferred to avoid icons for Web-browsing software they did not care to use were unable to buy Windows without Internet Explorer ready for use.[6] The court went on to speculate that more innovation would have happened if Microsoft had behaved differently.[7] And the court conjectured that, but for Microsoft's behavior, Netscape and Sun Microsystems' Java technologies *might* have opened the door to competition for PC operating systems *in the future*.[8] Apart from some rhetorical flourishes, that is all the court asserted.

How could the court stand at the brink of concluding that Microsoft, a key source of America's global leadership in information technology, had violated the antitrust laws without solid evidence that Microsoft's actions had, on balance, harmed consumers in the past or would in the future? The court did so by reaching into an antiquated antitrust tool kit for a rationale to condemn Microsoft and by giving short shrift to exculpatory evidence.

First, the court accepted the use of traditional antitrust tests for monopoly power despite wide and varied evidence that Microsoft's market position, like most category leadership positions in the software industry, was fragile. Second, the court accepted backward-looking market definitions in a rapidly evolving industry and seems to have accepted the government's demonization of Microsoft employees as arrogant bullies. That led the court to confuse hard competition with predatory behavior. Third, the court concluded that Microsoft had prevented Netscape from distributing Navigator—in the parlance of antitrust, that it had "foreclosed" market access—despite exceptionally strong evidence to the contrary.

The case should have turned on whether Microsoft had exploited market power to the detriment of consumers. Instead, the case came down to two competing explanations for Microsoft's conduct. Both explanations accept Windows' role as the leading software *platform* for Intel-compatible PCs. A platform provides developers of applications software with services they can use instead of writing new computer code. For example, programs written for Windows can use Windows to instruct the computer's modem to dial a telephone number. Windows is popular with consumers in part because many high-quality applications have been written to run with it.

But agreement ends there.

According to Microsoft, the company's actions are best characterized as vigorous competition over software platforms. Netscape's Web-browsing software had the potential to become an Internet-centric platform by itself or in combination with Java. To contend with that competitive threat and to respond to the Internet explosion, Microsoft developed its own Web-browsing software and integrated it into Windows to maximize Windows' value to consumers and to provide an Internet-enabled platform for developers. As part of that strategy, Microsoft also distributed its Web-browsing software aggressively. The strategy worked in large part because Internet Explorer (IE) was a better platform for applications developers than Navigator and at least as good a browser for consumers. Some of Microsoft's contracts, offering marketing preferences to distributors of Internet Explorer in return for preferential access to their customers, may have appeared problematic, but the contracts did not harm competition.

According to the government, Microsoft attempted to crush Netscape and Java to maintain the "applications barrier to entry" that protected the company's dominance in PC operating systems. That barrier allegedly arose because consumers would only use the platform with the most applications, and software developers would only write applications for the most popular platform. The government argued that Microsoft aimed to monopolize markets for

PC operating systems and browsers, not to maintain its leadership in software platforms. Microsoft did so by tying the sale of its browser to the sale of its operating system, by "selling" its browser at a price of zero, and by employing restrictive contracts. Oddly, the government did not claim that Microsoft sought to maintain its leadership—or monopoly—in software platforms.

This case has many subsidiary issues of legal significance—among them whether a browser and a computer operating system are best viewed as separate products or whether both Navigator and Internet Explorer are really platforms resting on operating systems. In addition is the legal question of whether it is predatory to improve a product and give the improvements away for free. But despite the government's evident preference to focus attention elsewhere, the central question in the case is what effect such behavior has had on consumers—in particular, whether Microsoft expanded its share of browser users in a way that harms consumers. For a firm can only violate the antitrust laws if it has victimized consumers.

In the following section we describe the main Microsoft actions at issue—the browser wars with Netscape and Microsoft's response to the challenge posed by Sun's Java technologies. Then, we analyze the government's definition of the relevant markets and its allegation that Windows made Microsoft a monopolist. After examining the main conduct to which the government objected—Microsoft's integration of Web-browsing functionality into Windows and its contracts with various parties to distribute Internet Explorer to the exclusion of Navigator—we consider how the court concluded that Microsoft undermined competition without finding that its actions have hurt or will hurt consumers.

Internet-Driven Platform Competition

Microsoft and the government agreed that Microsoft competed vigorously with Netscape and Java. Here, we describe

Microsoft's actions and their consequences without attempting to assess whether those actions "went too far."

Operating Systems, Platforms, and Middleware. To understand the case, it is important to understand the distinction between operating systems and software platforms. *Platform* software provides standardized modules of code that software developers can use to avoid the costly job of re-creating code to perform routine operations. For example, applications writers can use code in Windows, the MacOS, or Linux to control printing instead of writing specialized "drivers" for a host of printers. Platforms give software developers access to those modules of code by making available (or "exposing") "applications programming interfaces" or APIs, which provide links between the application code and the platform code.

All else equal, a platform is more attractive to consumers, the more high-quality applications are written to run on it. (Other factors, such as stability and ease of use, also matter.) Thus, an important aspect of competition among platforms—the critical aspect in the government's view of the case—is competition for the attention and allegiance of applications software developers. The more useful the features a platform provides to software developers, the easier it will be to write high-quality applications for that platform and the more such applications will be written. And, of course, the more popular a platform is with end-users, the more attractive it will be to applications developers. Software platforms may compete vigorously for applications even though, from the computer user's point of view, the platforms are not good substitutes for each other.

Most software platforms are *operating systems*—examples include Windows, Linux, OS/2, and the MacOS. The core task of an operating system is to tell the computer hardware what to do—for example, to store and retrieve information, to display characters on a monitor, or to use a modem to connect to the Internet. And since operating systems can provide those same services to applications, an operating system is often a good software platform.

Much of this case involves competition between Microsoft's Windows platform, which is an operating system, and platforms that are themselves applications software. Those so-called "middleware" platforms metaphorically stand between an operating system and other software applications and extend services to those applications. For example, Lotus Notes, a popular software application built to run on a number of operating systems, can be used as a platform for other sorts of software applications. If an application used only the services provided by Lotus Notes, it could run on any operating system on which Notes could run. And if Notes were able to capture the allegiance of a large number of applications developers in that fashion, it would become more valuable to consumers, while the operating systems on which it ran would become correspondingly less valuable.

The World Wide Web itself provides yet another type of platform for applications software. The Web consists of "servers" operating on widely agreed standards that make information—and, increasingly, applications software—available to end-users over the public communications network. Those standards, by which the servers move around information that is intelligible to consumers on their PCs, effectively define a software platform.

Software developers can write applications that run on the server and that can be used, over the Web, by anyone with a browser that complies with Internet standards. For instance, most broad-based Internet portal sites—among them Lycos, Yahoo!, Netcenter, and America Online—now offer calendar programs that store and display individual users' schedules. One can gain access to his calendar with almost any browser running on any operating system. The more high-quality "Web-based" applications of this sort that are written, the less valuable specific PC operating systems become to consumers—whose primary interest, after all, is efficient access to good applications software.

Figure 2-1 shows the relationships among hardware, operating systems, platforms, middleware, the Web, and software applications. The platform model on the left is based on the marriage between a specific operating system and type of hardware. The platform model in the center is based on middleware that can sit on top of many different operating system–hardware combinations. The platform model on the right is based on applications that run from the server and connect with client computers running many different operating system–hardware combinations.

The government and Microsoft agreed that Windows was an operating system that served as a platform; that Netscape Navigator was middleware that could evolve into a competitive platform; and that Java posed a middleware platform threat that was enhanced because it was widely distributed with Navigator.

Browser as Middleware. The commercial potential of the Internet became apparent during the early 1990s. Senior executives at Microsoft recognized that the Internet was a significant opportunity—and a significant threat—during 1993 and 1994.[9]

The Internet expanded the market for platform software—notably Windows—since the growing value of the Internet would make more people want to use computers. And that, in turn, would increase the demand for Internet-oriented platform features and services that developers could use for writing new applications.

But the Internet was also a technological discontinuity that threatened Windows' established position. Other Internet-friendly platforms might draw applications writers away from Windows. For example, IBM announced before Microsoft that it was adding Web-browsing software to its operating system (OS/2).[10] Or, as discussed above, consumers could migrate to Web-based applications that could be used with almost any computer. Or rivals could gain control of the communication and language standards for the Internet and leave Microsoft at a severe competitive disadvantage.

FIGURE 2-1
THREE TYPES OF SOFTWARE PLATFORMS: OPERATING SYSTEMS, MIDDLEWARE, AND THE WEB

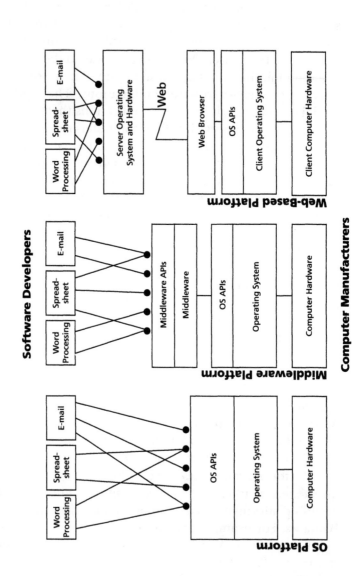

Microsoft's response was to develop new Internet-related technologies and to promote their use. In 1993 Microsoft decided to incorporate Internet features into the next generation of its software platform.[11] Many of those features involved the basic technologies and standards for connecting PCs to the Internet. Microsoft also decided to include Web-browsing software that would enable users to locate and view material on the Internet. Because Microsoft's internal efforts to develop browsing code did not proceed rapidly enough for inclusion in the release of Windows 95, Microsoft licensed code from Spyglass late in 1994 and used it as the basis for the first two versions of Internet Explorer (IE).[12]

Netscape was incorporated in April 1994 and released the first version of its Navigator browser software in December 1994. Navigator was an immediate hit and rapidly displaced earlier browsers. Navigator's success was due to its superior performance—and to Netscape's decision to distribute most copies free of charge via the Internet.[13] Navigator's market position was essentially unaffected by Microsoft's release of IE 1 as part of Windows 95 in August 1995, most likely because reviewers and consumers poorly received IE 1.

As part of its business strategy for defending and increasing the value of Windows, Microsoft wanted software developers (including developers of content for the Web) to use the Internet functionality built into Windows. But developers would not rely on Windows' browser technologies if consumers were not using them. And Internet users would see less value in Windows if new software did not rely on IE. That made it important for Microsoft to distribute IE technologies widely, even beyond the distribution of the Windows platform.[14]

In 1995 some Netscape executives suggested that their company would turn Navigator into an Internet-enabled middleware platform that could erode the value of Windows. They implied that future versions would include a rich menu of services for software developers and that Netscape would make a serious effort to get software developers to use those services. Microsoft executives viewed that as a credible strategy for the firm with the dominant browsing software.[15] They thus took quite seriously Netscape founder Marc Andreessen's repeated threat to reduce Windows to a "slightly buggy set of device drivers"[16]—that is, to eliminate its special appeal as a software platform. They were also concerned when Netscape sponsored conferences aimed at persuading software developers to write applications for Navigator.[17]

Microsoft responded by investing heavily in browsing software and in persuading consumers to use it. IE 2 offered some improvements over IE 1, but most of Microsoft's efforts went into brand new browsing software that would be tightly integrated into Windows. The results were IE 3 (released in August 1996 as part of a Windows 95 update) and IE 4 (released with yet another Windows 95 update in September 1997).[18] Those efforts cost about $100 million a year in research and development.[19]

Microsoft and Netscape competed for two audiences: consumers and applications developers. Microsoft began to gain ground in the battle for consumers in late 1996. According to independent reviewers, IE 1 and IE 2 were inferior to Navigator 1 and 2, IE 3 was about equal to Navigator 3, and IE 4 was superior to Navigator 4.[20] And Microsoft gained the allegiance of applications developers with better technology. IE 3 was provided in component form that was easy and efficient to use as a platform. Netscape never developed a similar modular design to provide the broad set of features necessary for a software platform. Thus, despite Andreessen's threats and a few noisy conferences, Netscape never seriously competed with Microsoft for the attention of software developers.

In August 1996, when Microsoft released the first version of IE that was arguably as good as Navigator, Netscape was the main browser for at least 57 percent of all users and close to 80 percent of users who did not subscribe to AOL or other online services. Most online service subscribers still used older proprietary browsers, such as AOL's Booklink.[21]

Microsoft also stepped up its distribution efforts. Initially, Microsoft relied primarily on sales of Windows for distributing IE, with free upgrades available through download. But late in 1995, AOL decided to replace its proprietary browser and solicited offers from both Microsoft and Netscape. In March 1996, even though AOL and Microsoft's online service (MSN) were bitter rivals, Microsoft was given the nod: AOL agreed to distribute the forthcoming IE 3 as the browser of choice for its subscribers.[22]

Three factors explain Microsoft's success with AOL. First, IE's modular form made it easier for AOL to integrate IE technologies into the software it provided to subscribers.[23] Second, Microsoft agreed to distribute AOL software with Windows and to put a sign-up icon in an online services folder on the Windows' virtual desktop.[24] Third, Netscape offered little technical help to AOL and failed to leverage its unique assets. For example, as part of an agreement to use Netscape's technology, AOL wanted to manage Netscape's very popular portal site. But Netscape declined.[25]

Within a year of the release of AOL's IE-based software in the fall of 1996, most AOL subscribers were using it. Online service subscribers switching from "other" browsers accounted for the bulk of IE's gains in usage in 1996 and much of 1997. Under their agreements with Microsoft, the online services could not promote Netscape. Nevertheless, the fraction of their subscribers who employed Netscape rather than the default browsers provided by the services (about one in five) did not fall after the agreements took effect.[26]

Microsoft also entered into distribution agreements with Internet service providers (ISPs). In September 1996 the company offered ISPs the Internet Explorer Access Kit, which provided them with an easy means to customize and brand Internet Explorer.[27] In return for making IE their "preferred browser," Microsoft gave ISPs the right to use the kit at no charge. The license agreements contained no restrictions on the right of ISPs to distribute another browser. Netscape did not offer similar software until June 1997 and initially charged $1,995 for it.[28]

Microsoft also included ten ISPs in the "Internet Connection Wizard" within Windows 95, beginning in August 1996. Those ISPs agreed to meet targets for shipping IE, but they were able to distribute other browsers to customers who asked for them.[29] Microsoft voluntarily waived the allegedly restrictive portions of those contracts in April 1998.[30]

With the major improvements in IE 3, purchasers of new computers with Windows 95 installed were more likely to use IE, although most still chose Netscape until IE 4 came out. Microsoft enforced its rights under the Windows copyright and required computer makers ("original equipment manufacturers" or OEMs) to leave the IE icon on the Windows desktop that the user saw when a new computer was turned on for the first time.[31] OEMs could, however, install additional browsers before shipment and could even set Netscape or another browser as the default means of Web access in Windows as long as they left the IE icon visible. (Note that the user could delete the IE icon at any time, a process that takes just a few seconds.)

Meanwhile, Netscape's strategies were evolving in response both to Microsoft and to changing views on how to make money from the Internet. Microsoft's introduction of a browser (IE 3) that was both at least as good as Netscape's and available for free made it increasingly difficult for Netscape to charge for Navigator. Netscape ceased trying to charge anyone for its browsing software soon after IE 4 came out. Netscape found, however, that it could profit handsomely from selling advertising on Netcenter, the "portal" that Navigator users visited by default when they logged onto the Internet. The company began earning significant advertising revenues, which supplemented its substantial receipts from selling products and services to business customers.

Although Microsoft had been worried that Netscape would transform Navigator into a competing platform, little evidence exists from either the trial or from Michael Cusumano and David Yoffie's intensive interviews with Netscape employees that Netscape ever seriously planned to do so.[32] James Barksdale, for example, suggested in testimony that Andreessen's comment about "slightly buggy device drivers" reflected his youth and a "spirit of jocularity and sometimes sarcasm that have gotten us in trouble."[33] As of today, Netscape does not offer a modular browser, let alone a full-featured platform on which software developers can rely. Nonetheless, AOL purchased Netscape in March 1999 for AOL stock that had a market value of about $10 billion at the time the deal was consummated.[34]

Microsoft's overall share of browser users increased from 8 percent in the second quarter of 1996 to 56 percent three years later, while Netscape's decreased from 53 percent to 40 percent over the same period.[35] Other browsers virtually disappeared, as AOL and the other online services incorporated IE technology into their access software and other older browsers were replaced by new versions of IE or Navigator. Despite some controversy in the trial record about sources of data on browser use, the following facts do not appear to be in significant dispute:

- Microsoft's share, including AOL subscribers who use IE technologies branded by AOL, reached parity with Netscape in mid-1998 and had climbed to about 56 percent in the second half of 1999 at the conclusion of trial testimony.
- Netscape's share of new browser users is around 35 percent. So, in the absence of major innovations, we can expect Netscape's share of

all users to continue to decline to about that level.[36]

• Online service subscribers who use a version of IE branded by their services account for roughly 20 percent of browser users—more than one-third of IE's total share.

• AOL's contract with Microsoft expires in January 2001. If AOL chooses to replace Microsoft's IE technology in AOL's subscriber software with AOL's own Netscape technology, Netscape's share of browser use would substantially exceed Microsoft's share.[37]

Java Technologies as Middleware. Sun launched its Java platform in May 1995. Java's linked technologies give software developers the flexibility to write applications that can run on many different platforms. Software developers can use the Java programming language to write applications. They can also use features and services provided by Java "class libraries." A Java compiler translates Java instructions written by humans into Java bytecode that looks like computer gibberish.

Java software developers distribute their programs to users in the form of bytecode. To execute those programs, the user's computer must have a "Java runtime environment," which includes the class libraries mentioned above and a Java Virtual Machine (JVM)—software specific to the computer operating system that translates bytecode into instructions the computer operating system understands. The Java runtime environment thus provides a middleware platform for software developers.

Sun saw the Web as an especially attractive complement to its new technologies since Java applications downloaded from the Web would run on any computer with a Java runtime environment—which included every computer using Navigator as a browser. Sun also trumpeted Java as a major competitive challenge to Windows. Microsoft took the Java threat seriously: if Java succeeded, software developers would write applications to Java and not to Windows and thereby diminish the value of Windows.

Sun's Java strategy, however, confronted the same problem as other "high-level" programming languages (such as Algol, Fortran, Basic, and C) that had been introduced earlier as "cross-platform" solutions for mainframes, minicomputers, and personal computers. Developers face a tradeoff between using only the generic features of the programming language (which allow it to run on any operating system with no changes to the source code)[38] and taking advantage of platform-specific features (which can increase functionality and speed). The more sophisticated the application and its interface, the greater the attraction of choosing performance over portability. As a result, most major commercial applications make heavy use of platform-specific features.

Microsoft faced a dilemma in deciding whether to include a Java runtime environment with Windows. On the one hand, Java was getting a great deal of attention. It was a good language for writing Internet "applets" (small applications) suitable for downloading, and it had other advantages as well. So Windows would be more useful with a high-quality Java development kit and a JVM optimized for Windows. On the other hand, Java was being developed as a competing platform that, if successful, could reduce the value of Windows.

Microsoft obtained a license from Sun to develop a JVM for Windows. In April 1998, *PC Magazine* awarded Microsoft its Editor's Choice award, noting that "[f]or the second year in a row, Microsoft has produced the fastest and most reliable Java implementation. . . . The Microsoft Java environment has come close to a perfect score on our compatibility tests."[39] Those tests involved programs that Sun had certified as "pure" Java, which are supposed to run on any JVM. Yet Microsoft's Windows JVM beat out Sun's own JVMs running on both Windows and Sun's Solaris platform.

But Microsoft's standard Java runtime environment did not include Sun's method for making use of platform-specific computer code. Thus, Java programs that linked to Windows by using Sun's method would not run on a "stock" version of Microsoft's Java runtime environment for Windows. In addition, Microsoft added its own methods to Java for using Windows-specific APIs and other programs. Those additional features increased the attraction of writing Java applications targeted specifically at Windows. Java programs that make use of platform-specific elements, whether they use Sun's or Microsoft's approach to access them, are no longer fully cross-platform.

Sun alleged that Microsoft's actions violate both Microsoft's license agreement and the antitrust laws. The judge also was perturbed that Microsoft required developers who wanted the benefits of "First-Wave" agreements to make their Java applications compatible with Microsoft's JVM.[40] The government did not, however, offer evidence that any developers were "fooled" into using features specific to Microsoft's JVM when they were trying to write "pure" Java that could run on any platform. And vendors started adding new features to their versions of computer languages long before Java existed. The March 12, 1998, issue of *PC Week* argued:

> It's not supportable to accuse Microsoft of twisting Java to its own ends, because all of the Microsoft-specific extensions to Java in Visual J++ 6.0 can be disabled by simple selections of options. Developers who just want to write good Java that runs on any compatible platform will still find VJ++ 6.0 a well-crafted development system.[41]

It is worth noting that those disputes do not affect "pure" Java applications that do not rely on platform-specific code. Moreover, under an order from the court hearing Sun's suit, Microsoft has modified its standard JVM so that it can run Java programs that use Sun's method to access Windows features.

All commercially significant operating systems include (or, in the case of the BeOS, are about to include) Java runtime environments, often with JVMs developed by the operating system vendor. As a result, almost all new microcomputers can run Java applications out of the box. In addition, JVMs are widely distributed with browsers and other software, so that end-users have easy access (at no extra cost) to JVMs from several vendors.

Nevertheless, Java has yet to fulfill its "write once, run anywhere" promise. Java programs are slower than those written to specific platforms. As a result, while many "applets" are available for Java, no large successful desktop applications exist.[42] Faster hardware and server-based approaches are helping Java overcome those problems, although there is no guarantee that Java will ever become a leading platform.

Market Definition and Monopoly Power

Microsoft took a series of steps to develop an Internet-enabled platform that would appeal to both consumers and software developers. The firm had the leading platform for Intel-compatible computers, and it wanted to have the leading platform for software connecting to the Internet. If it succeeded, it would increase the sales of its platform (Windows) and benefit financially. If it failed, its core business would be imperiled.

This description of Microsoft's actions between 1994 and the present does not imply that all Microsoft's actions benefited consumers and were procompetitive. But it has far different implications for interpreting the economic evidence from the description advanced by the government.

Market Definition, Entry Barriers, and Deceptive Labeling. Microsoft portrayed itself as competing hard to remain the leading software *platform*, while the government portrayed it as illegally attempting to prevent the creation of a middleware platform that would increase competition

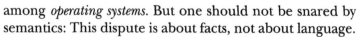

among *operating systems*. But one should not be snared by semantics: This dispute is about facts, not about language. The trial record is replete with evidence that Microsoft was deathly afraid of platform competition. All the business players in this drama recognized that they were battling for the allegiance of software developers in a race to provide the most attractive Internet-enabled platform. The government presented no evidence that Microsoft was worried that a competing *operating system* for Intel PCs was about to surface, and analysts and the trade press that follows the industry offer no visible support for that view.

Thus, on its face, the government's case has to be about platforms—not about operating systems and browsers. The government argues that Windows' monopoly power rests on the "applications barrier to entry," which deals entirely with competition among *platforms* for applications developers. Indeed, "protecting the applications barrier to entry" became the government's mantra in describing Microsoft's actions to defend its market position. And it became the theme of the court's findings of fact, with variations on that phrase appearing more than eighty-five times.

By the same token, no one disputes that Microsoft feared competition for Windows from Netscape and Java—and that the only thing all three have in common is their role as *platforms*. Normally in antitrust cases, markets are defined to include all products that impose significant competitive constraints on the product at issue. Since this case centers on Windows-related competitive responses to Netscape and Java, it is bizarre for the government to insist that both are outside the market that includes Windows.

Although no good *economic* reason exists for the government's refusal to focus on competition among platforms in this litigation, two good *tactical* reasons exist. First, looking systematically at platform competition makes it clear that the government's analysis of entry is inconsistent and thus that its analysis of monopoly power is fundamentally flawed. If the "applications barrier to entry" were truly formidable, neither Navigator nor Java could ever attract the allegiance of applications developers. Hence, the "applications barrier to entry" analysis, as presented by the government, implies that neither Netscape nor Java could ever pose serious competitive threats to Windows. But that is inconsistent with the undisputed reality that all companies involved believed that Netscape and Java were serious threats, despite their initial lack of applications. It follows that the "applications barrier" cannot be nearly so formidable as the government alleges.

The government never confronted that basic contradiction. It presented no evidence that Netscape and Java were uniquely capable of surmounting the barrier that it claimed protected Windows from the MacOS, OS/2, Linux, and other software platforms. The government claimed instead that middleware technologies have the potential to "erode" the applications barrier, which it links rhetorically to "the operating systems market." But that is nothing but a word game. Any platform, middleware or not, must develop a substantial stock of applications to be competitive.

Thus, Netscape and Java would have needed software developers to write applications for them and would have faced the same hurdles as other entrants into the platform arena.[43] The government ends up in the illogical position of claiming that an insurmountable barrier to platform entry exists while at the same time claiming that Microsoft had a powerful incentive to crush firms that wanted to surmount the barrier. The government's refusal to consider platform competition apparently hid that contradiction from the court.

The other tactical reason why the government refused to analyze competition among platforms consistently is that its focus on operating systems made it much easier to label two aspects of Microsoft's conduct as anticompetitive under antitrust case law. First, if browser software (Navigator and Internet Explorer) and Windows were distinct and complementary products, the government could claim that

Microsoft had "tied" browsing software (IE) to Windows because it would not offer them separately. If Windows and Navigator were both platforms, however, Microsoft's inclusion of browsing features in Windows would at first blush be no more surprising than Netscape's addition of many nonbrowsing features (such as e-mail software) to its market-leading browser.

Second, the government claimed that Microsoft engaged in predation by pricing IE at zero and spending heavily on distribution. But if Windows and Navigator are viewed as competitors in the platform market, the predatory pricing analysis would have to consider whether Microsoft's investment in and pricing and distribution of *Windows* (not IE) met the appropriate legal test for predation.[44]

And that would put the government in a deep hole. Predation generally involves incurring losses to extinguish competition. Yet Windows was highly profitable throughout the relevant period. It is therefore inconceivable that Microsoft could have been found guilty of predation in platforms. As Microsoft noted, even a tiny increase in Windows' sales would offset its investments in the development and distribution of IE.[45]

Thus, sophistry by misleading market definition is at the heart of the government's case. To see how important it is to the court's findings of fact, just replace the pejorative "protecting the applications barrier to entry" with the neutral "competing to be (or to remain) the leading platform." Allegedly anticompetitive actions like adding browsing features to Windows suddenly appear to be procompetitive. Microsoft's efforts to beat Netscape—which in 1996 claimed an 80 percent share of the crucial browser business[46]—are seen for what they really were: vigorous competition that benefited consumers.

Monopoly Power and the Applications Barrier to Entry. In casual conversation, few would dispute that Microsoft has at least a short-run monopoly over PC software platforms, even though consumers could opt for Apple computers and the MacOS, use OS/2, Linux, or the BeOS, or stick with old versions of Windows or MS-DOS forever. Microsoft has a "monopoly" in the everyday sense of that word because most people choose to buy Intel-compatible computers, and they generally demand the latest version of Windows to go with it. Similarly, nobody would deny that "barriers" exist that make it tough to get into the software platform business: one must come up with a product better than Windows for at least some purposes, and one must persuade consumers to buy it and software developers to write for it. Moving from a viable niche product to something that could displace Windows as the market leader would be even harder, in part because Windows already has lots of applications written for it.

But antitrust law demands more rigorous analysis. Economists usually define market power as the power to raise price above competitive levels. And since software products are highly differentiated, all successful software firms charge above marginal cost (which is usually trivial) and thus have some market power. Monopoly power, by contrast, is usually defined as substantial, long-lived market power.

The definition commonly cited by courts in antitrust cases is the "power to control prices or exclude competition."[47] Those alternative criteria amount to the same thing: to control prices (to hold them substantially above competitive levels) for a substantial time, a firm must be able to exclude competition. The only way a firm can exclude competition is by having some long-lived advantage that prevents other firms from competing effectively. Without such a barrier, monopoly power as defined in the antitrust context cannot exist—no matter how large a firm's market share or how great its short-run control over price.

In the software business, barriers to new, noninnovative products are frequently created by network effects (the more users or applications a product has, the more attractive it is to all) and a combination of switching costs and imperfect information (why go to the trouble of switching to a new product that offers no performance benefits but might have costly defects?).[48] Thus, it is unlikely that WordPerfect for DOS would ever have been displaced by a "me-too" word processor—one that could only have advertised "just as good but cheaper." But WordPerfect *was* displaced, by a product described by reviewers and perceived by consumers as better. Indeed, the history of PC software has been one of successful entry by innovative products,[49] and no evidence that the pace of software innovation is slowing exists. Accordingly, any analysis of barriers to entry in software platforms must focus on the competition that matters—and ask whether any barriers would prevent an *innovative* entrant from competing effectively.

Put another way, because the antitrust laws are about protecting consumers, a useful economic definition of a barrier to entry here is something that prevents innovative entry that would make consumers better off. The distinction between innovative and "me-too" entry is critical. Network effects, on which the government's "applications barrier to entry" rests, may indeed be an important reason why Windows is not likely to be threatened by "me-too" entry, especially in light of Microsoft's widely acknowledged low-price, high-volume strategy. But no support exists for the idea that such network effects retard the adoption of *innovative* products that provide new features consumers value. And innovative products have never been in short supply in the software business.[50]

The theoretical and empirical basis for the applications barrier to entry. The court cited only one reason why Microsoft could exclude entry and therefore had monopoly power in the legal sense: it found that the "applications barrier to entry" enabled Microsoft to control prices by preventing the development of a commercially viable alternative to Windows.[51] Certainly, most consumers use Windows partly because it has more applications written for it than any other competitive platform. That stock of applications, the court's reasoning goes, prevents entry by other operating systems because software developers have no incentive to write for those other operating systems.

But that is like saying that because incumbent firm A has a factory and B does not, B is prevented from competing by a "factory barrier to entry." The relevant question is whether any barrier prevents B from building a factory or, in this case, whether innovative new platforms can attract applications program developers and thus build a stock of applications over time.

The court made five assertions to support its view that an "applications barrier to entry" existed:[52]

> There is a "collective-action" problem. Independent software vendors will not write applications unless other ISVs [independent software vendors] write applications—and so no one writes them.

> Even an operating system with several thousand applications would be a "gamble" to adopt for consumers who could use Windows with its 70,000 applications.

> It would be prohibitively expensive for a fledgling operating system to persuade enough ISVs to write applications.

> The MacOS is not "a viable substitute for Windows" because it has *only* 12,000 applications.

> The applications barrier to entry prevented IBM's OS/2 from competing with Windows because IBM could not attract enough developers.

None of those assertions touches on the central question of whether the difficulty in getting software developers to write applications prevents consumers from getting a better product at a lower price. In referring to the "collective-action problem," the court identified the sort of chicken-and-egg problem that free markets have solved many times. Nintendo displaced Atari in games, even though consumers had Atari machines for which many games had already been written. The Sony PlayStation later succeeded despite Nintendo's huge installed base. Electricity replaced steam power, even though no distribution grid existed when the dynamo was invented. Automobiles replaced horses-and-buggies, even though no gas stations initially existed and the stocks of both horses and buggies were large. CDs replaced vinyl records, even though initially little music was available on CDs and virtually no one owned CD players. In the early days of the PC business, MS-DOS displaced CP/M, even though CP/M had many more applications. Consumers and producers of complements will gamble on upstarts if the potential prize is large enough.

Most industries based on goods that complement each other or that connect with each other over a network encounter chicken-and-egg problems. To succeed in those industries, businesses must innovate and develop marketing strategies to solve such problems. Many software developers for the Web try to establish their software as a de facto standard by giving away the basic version. The resulting base of users increases the demand for and supply of complementary products.

Netscape used that strategy when it gave away Navigator to almost all consumers. Apple has followed a similar approach with its video software QuickTime, which is available free for the Windows platform as well as for the MacOS. Similarly, Adobe gives away Acrobat Reader, and RealNetworks gives away RealPlayer. And, of course, Microsoft gives away Internet Explorer for the MacOS as well as for Windows. The facts cited by the court do not support its view that the chicken-and-egg problem in platforms cannot be overcome by intelligently marketing an innovative product.

The court said that Apple with its 12,000 applications and OS/2 with 2,500 applications had not succeeded in competing with Microsoft with its 70,000 applications.[53] But the reasons for Apple's failure to become the dominant operating system are well documented and little disputed— and have nothing to do with an applications barrier to entry.[54] Apple decided early in its history to sell integrated hardware and software packages and not to license its operating system to computer manufacturers.[55] Microsoft, by contrast, licensed its operating systems to computer makers that used Intel-compatible microprocessors and thus stimulated the development of a highly competitive and efficient market for hardware that has benefited consumers. Apple's vertically integrated strategy resulted in substantially higher prices for Apple computer systems than for IBM-compatible PC systems using MS-DOS, Windows, or other operating systems. Apple garnered far fewer sales than Intel-compatible vendors, despite what many felt was initially superior technology, and it sacrificed the network effects that proved so important to the rise of the Intel-compatible industry.

Microsoft introduced Windows in 1985, but it achieved little success during its first five years. Most observers expected OS/2, initially a joint effort by IBM and Microsoft released in 1987, to be the operating system for the next generation of PCs.[56] The first graphical version of Lotus 1-2-3, the dominant spreadsheet of the time, was written for OS/2. Similarly, the WordPerfect Corporation, which had the dominant word processing software, initially focused its graphical development efforts on OS/2—not on Windows. IBM placed its bets on OS/2, while Microsoft concentrated on promoting Windows, initially without much success.

To provide key business applications for Windows, Microsoft adapted Word and Excel from the Macintosh, where they had established themselves as the leaders in their categories. With the release of Windows 3.0 in 1990, Microsoft's investment finally began to pay off. But the battle with OS/2 (for which IBM assumed ownership following the 1990 "divorce" from Microsoft) continued for several years, with IBM advertising that OS/2 was a "better Windows than Windows."[57] Industry observers generally agree that OS/2 eventually failed for a variety of technical and strategic reasons unrelated to an "applications barrier to entry."[58]

The claim that software developers would not write applications to fledgling operating systems is also inconsistent with the reality that software developers are actively writing applications to Linux and the MacOS and developing the Web-based applications discussed in the previous section. Most applications programmers now write for multiple platforms.[59] The number of applications for Linux is increasing steadily.[60] Applications written for the MacOS have also increased sharply with the resurgence of Apple's sales after the introduction of its iMac line of computers.[61] And the number of Web-based applications is increasing dramatically.[62]

Similarly, investors do not seem to believe that it is impossible to compete with Windows. Investment capital is pouring into promising new platforms—Linux, the MacOS, Java, and the Web. Between the time that testimony ended in June 1999 and the end of the year, several companies that specialize in Linux went public, including Red Hat and VA Linux. Those two companies were offered initially at a combined market capitalization of $2.15 billion in the fall of 1999. By the end of the year, they were valued at over $22.7 billion.[63]

Does Microsoft act as if an insurmountable barrier protected it? Just as other market participants act as if the applications barrier to entry is low and porous, so does Microsoft. As discussed above, Microsoft's massive investments to compete with Netscape and other potential Web-centric platforms, as well as its concern about Java, are inconsistent with the government's theory of an impenetrable barrier. The government never resolved that inconsistency. Nor did it explain why Microsoft invests so much in attracting developers to the Windows platform if, as its theory implies, it can always count on developers writing to the most popular platform. Testimony at trial showed that Microsoft devotes about 2,000 employees and $650 million each year to attracting and supporting applications developers.[64] If a serious applications barrier to entry exists, such an investment is pure waste from Microsoft's perspective.

By the same token, the government never tested its theory with data or tried to quantify consumer losses from Microsoft's exercise of monopoly power. The government's theory implies that Microsoft can price Windows without regard to possible future competition. Indeed, the protected monopolist described by the government could charge at least $900 under very conservative assumptions.[65] Yet Microsoft on average charges computer manufacturers about $65 for Windows 95/98—a mere 4 percent of the average price paid for the hardware in the average system and far less than the price of many software applications.[66]

The government offered no substantive response to that contradiction. The Department of Justice's economist, Franklin M. Fisher, simply dismissed it. He said that the analysis showed only that Microsoft was not charging the short-run profit-maximizing price for Windows.[67] That statement does not square with the government's theory, however. If a durable, impenetrable barrier to entry protected Windows, Microsoft would have no reason to charge anything lower than the short-run profit-maximizing price. Indeed, the government's economists went so far as to say that a rational firm should charge the most it can today and lower prices only if entry actually occurs.[68]

Did Microsoft Really Behave Badly?

Suppose now, for the sake of argument, that Windows did give Microsoft monopoly power in software platforms. It is not generally illegal for a monopolist to respond to competition, even if it intends to retain its monopoly and succeeds in doing so. Nor does that generally harm consumers. For instance, a monopolist can legally solidify its dominance by reducing costs so that it can profitably cut prices in the face of competition. It can seek to raise the quality of its product to a level that its competitors cannot match. Consumers would be worse off if a monopolist opted instead for the quiet life and declined to defend its position.

It is, however, generally illegal for a monopolist to compete in ways that both enhance its power and make consumers worse off. A firm in a competitive market that burns a rival's plant commits arson. A monopolist that does so also violates antitrust laws. While Microsoft did compete to defend its market position, none of the actions to which the government objects has harmed consumers or is likely to do so.

In the first prong of its case against Microsoft's conduct, the government charged that Microsoft's "tying" of Internet Explorer to Windows was a per se violation of the antitrust law—an action that is illegal regardless of its consequences. The government also charged that Microsoft invested in developing and distributing IE solely to destroy Navigator and cripple Java and that its provision of IE for free as an integral part of Windows was thus predatory.

In the second major prong of its case, the government charged that Microsoft foreclosed Netscape and Sun from distributing their software in two ways. First, Microsoft prevented Netscape from getting Navigator into the hands of consumers who bought new computers by integrating IE into Windows and prohibiting OEMs from removing it.[69] Second, the company prevented Netscape from distributing Navigator through online service providers, Internet service providers, and Internet content providers by entering into restrictive contracts with many of those providers. Lacking distribution, Netscape fizzled.

Essentially no support for those charges exists. The tying allegation is an artifact of the government's misleading market definitions. So is the predation charge. Microsoft invested in improving its profitable software platform by adding features and functionality, as it had done ever since it released MS-DOS 1.0. After the investment, the platform was plainly better and still highly profitable.

We believe that neither economic theory nor antitrust case law provides any support for a policy that would condemn as predatory an investment in innovation that improves a profitable product—even one sold by a tough monopolist. Any such policy would chill innovation by leading firms, particularly in the software business where adding features and functionality is a major avenue of product improvement. Even under the government's expansive and dangerous definition of predation—which would label any forgone short-run profits as "losses"—the government introduced no evidence to show that Microsoft would have obtained higher profits by deviating from its long-standing policy of including new features in Windows without charging separately for them.

On the other hand, the foreclosure charge tells a consistent story that does not depend on the government's market gerrymandering. It is clearly illegal for a monopolist to prevent a competitor from distributing its product, and some of the Microsoft contracts look exclusionary. But the facts are singularly unkind to this story: an abundance of evidence shows that Netscape distributed its product widely through many channels, including those that the government said were closed to it. The most telling evidence came from information that Netscape provided to Goldman Sachs, which AOL hired in the fall of 1998 to conduct a "due diligence" inquiry into the value of Netscape. Goldman Sachs's presentation to AOL's board of directors concerning the multibillion-dollar merger flatly contradicted the key claims of the government and its economists. The court's findings of fact are silent on the Goldman Sachs material that was presented in detail during Microsoft rebuttal testimony in June 1999.

Finally, it is worth noting that despite what the government describes as the ruthless exercise of enormous power, Microsoft did not succeed in eliminating the competitive threat posed by Netscape and Java. Netscape is now part of AOL, which is highly profitable and whose 21.5 million subscribers (including those of AOL's subsidiary, CompuServe) generally use whatever browser AOL provides in its access software.[70] AOL is also formally allied with Sun, which has made its Java runtime environment ubiquitous. With adequate platform technology, either could seriously threaten Windows tomorrow.

Predation. The government said that Microsoft invested in the development and distribution of IE to prevent Netscape Navigator from becoming a successful platform. That is predation, said the government. Microsoft responded that it invested in the development and distribution of IE to help ensure that Windows remained a successful platform. That is competition, said Microsoft. This is a classic problem, since the line between predation and tough competition is hard to define in theory and even harder to draw in practice.[71]

Predation, like competition, increases quality and lowers prices. Successful predation leads to higher prices or lower quality or both only after the intended victim is vanquished—and only harms consumers if the postpredation costs imposed on them outweigh the benefits they received during predation.

Deciding where to draw the line is especially difficult before the alleged strategy has succeeded. Competition and predation look much the same during this period, especially in an industry where marginal costs are close to zero and free distribution is common. The government used Microsoft e-mails to argue that since Microsoft intended to smash Netscape and Java, its actions must have been predatory. But in a struggle to the death, the intent to kill is exactly the same as the intent to live. No matter how colorful, quotations from caffeine-fueled e-mails cannot separate the two. To distinguish predatory from competitive conduct, one must predict prices and quality after the alleged episode of predation ends. That is very hard to do. Most troublesome, mistakenly penalizing highly competitive firms inhibits competition and forces consumers to pay higher prices in both the present and the future.

Hence, in the past two decades the courts have set high standards for proving that behavior is predatory. In particular, the courts have required evidence that the alleged predator has a rational basis for believing that it will recoup its losses after its targeted rivals succumb. That, in turn, requires showing that eliminating today's rivals (Netscape and Java in this case) will ensure a substantial period of unchallenged monopoly. The government plainly found those standards troublesome and sought to skirt them by claiming that Microsoft was able to recoup its losses simultaneously in another market by maintaining its monopoly over operating systems for Intel-compatible computers.[72]

That novel "simultaneous recoupment" argument is inconsistent with other aspects of the government's case and with the court's findings of fact. The government never claimed in its proposed findings of fact that there would have been more competition in the market for operating systems between 1995 and 1999 if Microsoft had not sought to defeat Netscape and Java. And the court said that the evidence was insufficient to conclude that more competition would have existed during that time period. So any benefits Microsoft realizes from its predation must have been expected to materialize sometime in the future.

To test the government's predation theory, one has to ask whether Microsoft could reasonably have expected to recoup its alleged losses on IE.[73] We do not attempt to put ourselves into the minds of Microsoft executives when they were making the relevant decisions. Rather, we make three observations concerning the evidence and its interpretation.

First, the government claimed that Netscape Navigator would cease being a competitive threat when its market share fell below 50 percent. The only evidence in the record for that proposition is an e-mail from a Microsoft employee who tracked browser usage and suggested that Microsoft had won the browser war when Microsoft's share exceeded 50 percent.[74]

The court went further. It said that applications developers would not write for a platform if they believed that it would not become the dominant platform. As Netscape's share of all users and of incremental users fell below 50 percent, hope of its becoming the dominant platform vanished.

No evidence supports that theory. Indeed, according to the trial record, software developers are writing applications for Linux, the MacOS, and the Web.[75] Significant capital is flowing to companies that provide applications software and ancillary services to Linux users, although it would be rash for anyone to predict that Linux will become the next dominant platform. Everything in the record indicates that if Netscape had developed Navigator into a versatile platform, it would have attracted applications writers. But it did not develop competitive features and services for software developers.

Second, if Microsoft had a strategy to push Netscape's market share below 50 percent and keep it there, that strategy must have depended critically on assistance from AOL. If AOL had declined to use IE technologies instead of Navigator, Microsoft's and Netscape's current shares would be reversed, and Netscape would have a share in excess of 60 percent.[76]

In light of the history of bitter relations between AOL and Microsoft, the idea that Microsoft counted on long-term help from AOL to crush Netscape is far-fetched. Moreover, AOL now owns Netscape. It is hard to imagine that the benefit AOL gets from its place in the Windows online services folder is greater than the benefits it would earn by developing a middleware platform that earned even a modest fraction of Windows' profits. AOL may switch to Navigator in January 2001 (when it next has that option), develop Netscape software into an attractive, widely distributed middleware platform, and thereby defeat Microsoft's aims. Or AOL may stick with IE, in which case it must believe that a middleware platform strategy based on the browser is not worth pursuing—and that Microsoft's alleged predation strategy was thus unnecessary.

Third, the government claimed that Microsoft tried to reduce Netscape's share of browser use to make it a less effective vehicle for distributing Java technologies. The evidence indicates that browsers are only one of many ways to distribute the Java runtime environment. As noted above, current versions of virtually all desktop operating systems include the essential Java components, and Microsoft's version of the Java runtime environment has won awards for being compatible with more "pure" Java programs than either Sun's or Netscape's versions. While Microsoft and Sun continue to do battle in court about whether Microsoft is required to support Sun's approach to making use of platform-specific features, users of Windows can obtain alternative runtime environments at no cost through multiple channels. Sun may have a legitimate contract beef with Microsoft with respect to Java, but it is hard to see that dispute as an antitrust issue. And it is even harder to see how consumers are harmed if developers are given more tools and options for writing programs. Nor do we find it surprising (or reprehensible) that Microsoft expects its "First Wave" partners to write Java programs that work with Microsoft's JVM. The whole purpose of First Wave arrangements is to generate marketing benefits for both Microsoft and allied software developers.

The Government's Foreclosure Theory vs. the Evidence.
Readers may find that the government's foreclosure claims are inconsistent with their own experiences. Netscape Navigator was (and is) widely distributed and readily available to anyone wanting a copy. Many academics used Navigator

because their universities installed it on their systems, and it was freely available to copy for home use. Their students also had ready access to free copies of Navigator. Millions of people downloaded Navigator from Netscape's Web site or from thousands of other Internet sites. People who bought computers from several popular computer manufacturers received Navigator preinstalled. Many Internet service providers, including the Baby Bells, made Netscape readily available on CDs. All told, Netscape reported to Goldman Sachs that it distributed 160 million copies of Navigator in 1998.[77] That works out to about 1.6 copies for every Web user. And Goldman Sachs, in its long and thorough report to the AOL board (which was then considering the acquisition of Netscape), never suggests that Netscape has been prevented from distributing its flagship Navigator product.

The real explanation for Navigator's decline is quite simple. Despite the free distribution and presence of IE 1 and IE 2 on every new machine that had Windows 95, those IEs attracted few users because they were inferior to Netscape's offerings. IE 3 attracted more users because its reviews were roughly as good as those of Navigator 3 and because Microsoft won the competition to provide the browsing technology for AOL and other online services. IE 4 attracted an even larger market share because it was widely considered superior to Navigator 4.[78] Ironically, one of the advantages of IE 3 and IE 4 cited by many reviewers was their tight integration in Windows.

The Court's Findings of Fact. The court concluded otherwise. Doing so required the court to ignore clear evidence that Navigator was distributed widely through numerous channels—including the ones that the government claimed Microsoft had cut off.

Consider the court's finding that Microsoft had foreclosed Netscape from distributing its software through computer manufacturers. The only evidence backing that finding is testimony by the Justice Department's economist,

Professor Franklin Fisher: "By the beginning of January 1999, Navigator was present on the desktop of only a tiny percentage of PCs that OEMs were shipping."[79] But Netscape itself told Goldman Sachs in the fall of 1998 that Navigator was distributed on 22 percent of computers— even before it struck a deal in January 1999 to preinstall Navigator on all machines in Compaq's consumer line.[80]

Other evidence suggested that Netscape could have been on even more computers if it had chosen to focus on distribution through that channel. Before the release of Windows 95, James Barksdale told Microsoft that Netscape did not plan to develop the OEM channel as a primary source of distribution.[81] And contrary to the government's assertions that Netscape had achieved wide distribution on new computers before Microsoft's tightening of "first-screen" provisions in mid-1996, survey data show that, as of early 1996, only 6 percent of Navigator users had obtained Navigator with their computers. By the start of the trial, after several years of allegedly anticompetitive exclusion from the OEM channel, almost 20 percent of Navigator users reported obtaining their copies with their purchases of new computers.[82]

Consider next the court's finding that downloading had become an ineffective means of distribution. No quantitative evidence in the trial record supported that proposition. It is apparently based on the unsupported assertions of government witnesses. But the numbers tell a very different story. Netscape reported to Goldman Sachs that most of the 160 million copies it distributed in 1998 were downloaded.[83] Survey data showed that as of the third quarter of 1998, 18 percent of consumers who used browsers had obtained those browsers through downloading.[84] After the release of the much improved IE 3 in August 1996, the share of copies of IE obtained by downloading leapt from 16 percent to 49 percent.[85]

Back to Predation. Undoubtedly, Microsoft's development and aggressive distribution of a competitive browser made it harder for Netscape to persuade consumers to use its browsing software or to persuade third-party distributors to give away Navigator. There was, however, no evidence that consumers who wanted Navigator had difficulty obtaining it.[86]

According to survey data, Microsoft's share of browser users rose from 8 percent in the second quarter of 1996 (before the release of IE 3) to 57 percent in the second quarter of 1999 (a year and a half after the release of IE 4). The increases over the three intervening years coincided with AOL's decision to adopt IE technology (based in part on its modular design) and with dramatic increases in the quality of IE relative to Navigator. During that period, the total number of browser users increased by more than 56 million. Microsoft captured just over two-thirds of the increase, half of which included subscribers to AOL and other online services. Among other Web users, Microsoft captured about 56 percent of the increment, with the vast majority obtained after the release of IE 4 in October 1997—and after Microsoft voluntarily ended most of its allegedly anticompetitive contractual restrictions on distribution in April 1998.[87]

To achieve those gains, Microsoft invested in improving IE (and hence Windows) and in putting IE in the hands of consumers. Microsoft's investment in the modular design of IE, which AOL, the other online services, and independent software vendors found appealing, was also a factor in IE's increase in share and Netscape's relative decline.

Anyone who wanted Navigator could easily get it. The same is true for Java: JVMs are ubiquitous. And, while Java faces many challenges, the distribution of Java runtime environments is not one of them—at least not according to any evidence introduced at trial or reported in the trade press.

The government's case focused on Internet browsing but brought in other "bad acts" by Microsoft to bolster its claims by demonizing Microsoft and its employees. The court devotes more than a dozen pages to incidents involving four companies: Intel, Apple, RealNetworks, and IBM, which it cites as evidence of Microsoft's "corporate practice to pressure other firms to halt software development that either shows the potential to weaken the applications barrier to entry or competes directly with Microsoft's most cherished software products."[88]

As with the browser-related claims, one looks in vain to find evidence of consumer harm. In three of the four cases, Microsoft's alleged pressure came to naught: Apple refused to stop developing and giving away QuickTime for Windows;[89] RealNetworks continued to develop and distribute basic multimedia streaming software;[90] and IBM refused to reduce promotion of its competing products to obtain the lower price of Windows it wanted from Microsoft.[91] Microsoft was successful in delaying the release of "Native Signal Processing" (NSP) software developed by Intel. But Microsoft's objections were based in large part on NSP's incompatibility with Windows 95, which Microsoft was about to release.[92] There were no corporate corpses here, and no consumers were hurt.

Where Did the Court Go Wrong?

Consumers have gotten cheaper and better browsing software as a result of Microsoft's actions. That accelerated the advance of the Internet revolution. Netscape Navigator is still widely used, is readily available, and has a powerful patron in its owner, the leading online service. Java is everywhere. Securities analysts and the trade press recognize that Microsoft Windows faces challenges from many directions, including Sun, Linux, and Web-based applications. Yet the government, encouraged by the court's findings that seem to put it firmly in the driver's seat, is apparently considering breaking up one of America's most widely admired and innovative companies; closely regulating its pricing, distribution, and product design; or both.

The only economic justification for such drastic actions would be the need to protect consumers from severe harm. But the court was unable to find that Microsoft's actions have on balance harmed consumers. As we noted at the outset, the court recognizes several tangible benefits from Microsoft's alleged predatory strategy: improving the quality of Web-browsing software, lowering its cost, and increasing its availability.[93]

People who wanted to use an operating system without an integrated browser may have incurred tangible costs. But the government introduced no evidence to show how many people objected to the presence of Internet Explorer or how much it would have been worth to them to be able to buy a browserless version of Windows. Because the marginal cost of including IE technologies as part of Windows is zero, a browserless and "full-strength" Windows might logically sell for the same price. Indeed, the states' economist, Frederick Warren-Boulton, suggested that Microsoft might have been justified in charging more for the browserless version to cover its incremental costs of developing the new product.[94] And if many copies of Windows had been distributed without the features available with IE technologies, applications writers who used them would have had to incur real costs to distribute IE with their products—or do without the platform services it provides.[95]

Other costs may have been incurred by consumers who would have benefited if computer manufacturers had the contractual right to customize the first screen that buyers see when they turn on their computers for the first time. But, again, the government offered no evidence. Clearly, the lost benefits could not have been large, because OEMs decided that consumers were not interested enough in customized screens to bother clicking an icon after the initial boot.[96] And even if the benefits of first-screen flexibility outweighed the costs, it is hard to believe that the net benefit would have exceeded the benefits of the better, cheaper software produced as a consequence of the browser wars.[97]

The court speculated that Microsoft's actions will, in the end, have harmed consumers by slowing innovation and limiting choice. But, once again, it is not possible to verify the court's conjectures. Consider, for example, the statement that there might be more innovation if Microsoft had not acted badly. Today, the capital markets are showering money on developers of Web-centric applications, Java applications, and Linux—all of which constitute challenges to Windows' platform dominance. And Apple is again attracting both consumers and applications writers. That does not absolutely, positively refute the court's theory that there would be more innovation but for Microsoft's conduct. But neither could any other evidence.

In the end, the court found that Microsoft had lowered prices, improved quality, and distributed IE widely. If the courts are to represent the interests of consumers, it is wrong to label the course of action that leads to those gains as predation.

How could the court have made the sweeping indictment of Microsoft contained in its findings of fact with so much evidence that Microsoft's actions have benefited consumers and so little evidence of consumer harm? And how could the government even consider draconian sanctions against a company whose major sin was developing better browsing software and including that software at no additional charge in the world's most popular operating system?

Part of the answer is that the government and the court are treating the software industry like the bricks-and-mortar industries from antitrust cases gone by.[98] Software firms benefit from scale economies and network effects that give them high shares in categories for which they provide the leading product. Those firms price their software well above marginal cost because copyright laws protect them from copycats—and because they must recover their development costs. But those firms' dominant positions are fragile because competition occurs through battles over innovation typically triggered by rapid technological change in hardware.

Firms compete with each other by developing new software features and functions, which they may release as new software products or combine with old ones. For example, Netscape's original browsing software (Navigator 1) evolved into a product (Communicator) that had capabilities to encrypt and decrypt e-mail, to set up and manage discussion groups, to create and edit Web pages, and to hold real-time Web conferences.[99] The government and the court thus confused the questions taught in elementary economics to detect departures from perfect competition—Are prices above marginal cost? Do firms have high market shares? Do they charge all customers the same price?—with an appropriate analysis of monopoly power in the software industry.[100]

Another part of the answer is that the government and the court used what Justice Cardozo once described as the "tyranny of tags and tickets."[101] Instead of asking whether Microsoft's actions harmed consumers—the modern touchstone of antitrust law—they tried to attach labels to those actions. To tag IE's inclusion in Windows as a tie, the government persuaded the court that it was possible for Microsoft to prevent its customers from gaining access to the browsing features in Windows. The implicit assumption was that Microsoft was somehow obliged to have designed a version of its product so that its distributors could prevent customers from using one of its most attractive new features. And the government's economists "proved" that a tie existed by "defining" a market for operating systems that excluded browsing and other platform features—although all major operating systems have included browsing features and touted the benefits of their integration.[102]

In all that, the government asserted its jurisdiction over the design of complex software products without ever enunciating a clear standard for legality or illegality. If that right to intervene is upheld, it will be a very dark day for the software industry—and for consumers.

Finally, the government and its economists tried to read Microsoft's corporate mind to show evil intent. Instead of conducting an empirical analysis of the effects of Microsoft's actions on competition or on Netscape's distribution costs, the government scoured Microsoft internal e-mails looking for sound bites that "showed" bad motives. But reading the minds of business executives to see whether they are seeking to compete with their rivals or seeking to harm their rivals is never an easy task, as the Justice Department's economist, Professor Fisher, recognized in an earlier case:

> The subjective intent of a company is difficult to determine and will usually reflect nothing more than a determination to win all possible business from rivals—a determination consistent with competition. . . . To premise their legality on an inquiry into the specific motivations of subjective intent of the firms that engage in such conduct (when it is clear that all firms engaged in competition attempt and intend to win as much business as they can) or on retrospective evaluation of whether there were more "desirable" alternative actions that could have been chosen, would be to elevate competitors above competition and threaten the entire competitive process for the sake of those who are not intended to be its beneficiaries and at the expense of those who are.[103]

It is particularly difficult to determine intent in a high-tech industry, in which e-mails are often unintelligible to anyone not privy to the technical and institutional context.

And it is essentially impossible to do so in an industry subject—as much of the software business is subject—to "winner-take-most" competition. Microsoft's intention to compete hard enough to maintain its market position *necessarily* entailed excluding Netscape from a major role in the platform business. Similarly, Marc Andreessen, a founder of Netscape, expressed his intention to compete in the platform business by repeatedly threatening to brush aside Windows.

Consumers benefit from that sort of brutal rivalry. They would be harmed if everyone competed nicely.

3

Misconceptions, Misdirection, and Mistakes

*Franklin M. Fisher and
Daniel L. Rubinfeld*

The chapter by David S. Evans and Richard L. Schmalensee is probably the most coherent version of the Microsoft defense that has yet been produced.[1] That does not mean that it is right, however. Indeed, it is filled with misconceptions, misdirection, and mistakes. Space does not permit a complete discussion, so we comment on a few major points, some of which we discussed at greater length in chapter 1.[2]

Consumer Harm

Evans and Schmalensee confuse the court's sensible caution in forecasting the future with a failure to find present harm, which the court most definitely found. While the court saw—as did Microsoft—a possible end to the Windows monopoly as a result of the new Internet technologies that Microsoft crushed, the court was not prepared to pull out a crystal ball and conclude that the Windows monopoly would definitely have ended by now if it were not for Microsoft's unlawful actions. But Microsoft's campaigns to limit competition, as the court rightly found, harmed consumers by denying them the fruits of innovation and the choice of alternative forms of computing in the Internet era. Microsoft did that to maintain its operating system monopoly.

Indeed, if nothing else—and there was more—the fact that the original equipment manufacturers (OEMs) felt injured by Microsoft's restrictions shows consumer harm. Because the OEMs compete with each other for consumer business, it is in their interest to offer products that are responsive to consumer demands. Restrictions *on original equipment manufacturers* thus restrict or limit consumer choice.

In any event, Evans and Schmalensee's position that a showing of *present* consumer harm is—or perhaps ought to be—a sine qua non for antitrust plaintiffs is all misdirection. That is not the law, nor is it good public policy or good economics.

Predatory campaigns can offer immediate consumer benefits. A firm that prices below cost to drive out rivals and earn or protect monopoly rents does so by offering consumers a deal that is, in effect, too good to be true. During such a campaign, consumers benefit from the low prices. If a showing of present consumer harm were required, no predator could be stopped until after the campaign was over, when it might well be too late to avoid substantial consumer harm.

Fortunately, the legal standard is otherwise. The presumption of antitrust policy is that competition itself brings consumer benefits, and the lessening of competition brings consumer harm. Hence, plaintiffs are required to show an injury to *competition* rather than immediate harm to consumers.

Market Definition and "Platform Competition"

Evans and Schmalensee argue that the government's case turned on a misconceived market definition and that, had it—and we—only perceived that the true competition was one of platforms rather than operating systems, the case would have fallen of its own weight. In fact, it is the Evans and Schmalensee argument that depends on a tortured market definition; ours is essentially independent of the market definition—as it should be.

According to Evans and Schmalensee, the government defined the market too narrowly, as including only PC operating systems. Their position is that, since Netscape's Navigator and Sun's Java—both middleware—provided platforms to which software developers could write applications, they were competing with Microsoft in the "platform market," and Microsoft's actions merely represented aggressive competition in that market.

First, as to market definition, the object of market definition in a monopoly case is—and ought to be—to provide the basis for an analysis of the constraints on an alleged monopolist's power. That means the constraints on its power in dealing with *buyers,* not the constraints on its dealing with the producers of complementary products. If Windows were and would remain the only *operating system* for Intel-based PCs, then every owner of a PC using Navigator or Java would of necessity require Windows. And that would be true regardless of how many applications were written for the middleware. Navigator and Java were *complements* to the operating system. Both also could facilitate the writing of applications that were also complements. They were not substitutes.

That does not mean that Navigator and Java presented no threat to Microsoft. On the contrary, they presented a threat that Microsoft greatly feared. If enough users acquired Navigator or Java, then applications writers might find it tempting to write for them. If that happened to a great enough extent, then it might not matter what operating system ran underneath them. In Microsoft's words, the operating system would become "commoditized," and the applications barrier to entry would be gone. Thus, Navigator and Java were facilitating devices that had the potential to aid the entry of competing operating systems. The competition that Microsoft feared would come from that entry and not directly from Navigator and Java.

Evans and Schmalensee's position is that the fact that Microsoft found it necessary to attack Navigator and Java must mean that those products were in the same market as Windows. But that is incorrect. Imagine that someone invented an automobile that would run on some fuel in addition to gasoline, say root beer. A monopolist of gasoline might well attempt to destroy that invention lest competition from root beer erode its monopoly position and profits. But one would hardly wish to say that the dual-fuel-driven *automobile* was in the same market as gasoline, even though its success could bring root beer into that market.

Second, the correct analysis should not be driven by the market definition. Theirs is, and ours is not. Even if one includes Navigator and Java in the same market as Windows, the analysis of Microsoft's actions would be basically the same. In that case, one would say that Microsoft took predatory actions to destroy two existing, if newborn, competitors who were introducing innovations that could lead to other entry.

Innovation to Enhance the Sale of Windows

It is not surprising that Evans and Schmalensee take the position that Microsoft's actions involved only product improvements that enhanced the sale of Windows. We discussed that in detail in chapter 1 and here only summarize some of the high points.

First, the browser is an important complement to the operating system. Microsoft had an interest in ensuring that consumers had a good browser that would work with Windows. But, if that were all, Microsoft would have no reason to spend hundreds of millions of dollars to ensure that the most heavily used browser would not be Netscape's.

Second, Microsoft spent considerable effort to force Apple to make IE the browser of choice. That cannot have contributed to the sale of Windows. As that suggests, Microsoft did not merely innovate and improve IE but forced on many others—for example, Apple, the Internet service providers, and the Internet content providers such as Intuit—restrictive agreements hampering the distribution and use of Navigator.

Third, one should not forget that Microsoft was not taking those actions because IE was a source of revenue. To the contrary, IE was a "no-revenue product." Microsoft sacrificed the ancillary revenues that IE might bring if an original equipment manufacturer or Internet service provider had wanted to feature a browser that used the IE technology under a different name and with a different portal site.

It is total misdirection to suggest that *Microsoft* was about improving the browser, or even primarily about integrating or bundling it into Windows. The case was largely about Microsoft's restrictive actions. Those included its refusal to offer Windows without IE—that is, to sell Windows both with and without IE. But far more than that was involved. Evans and Schmalensee seize on the court's praise of competition on the merits—yes, Microsoft did *some* of that in this period—and extend it to an exculpation of the entire anticompetitive scheme.

The Effect of Microsoft's Actions on Browser Shares

According to Evans and Schmalensee, Microsoft did not succeed in hampering Netscape and the threat it posed. They argue both that Netscape's distribution of Navigator continued to be extremely large and that Netscape's success is shown by the $4 billion purchase price offered by AOL when the deal was struck (not the $10 billion suggested by Evans and Schmalensee–this represents appreciation in the price of AOL stock). We can most charitably call both points misleading.

Evans and Schmalensee argue that Netscape continued to distribute its browser. They state: "Netscape reported to Goldman Sachs that it distributed 160 million copies of Navigator in 1998. That works out to about 1.6 copies for every Web user" (p. 78). But that second sentence should provide a clue that something is amiss. On that basis, every Web user has at least one, and many have more than one, copy of Navigator. On that basis, since IE is bundled with Windows, just about every PC user has IE as well.

The problem is that the possibility of reaching consumers with Navigator does not translate into reaching them effectively, into browser usage, or even into installation. Evans and Schmalensee claim that Netscape was not foreclosed by Microsoft's actions. For example, Microsoft did not prohibit original equipment manufacturers from installing Navigator in addition to IE, and Netscape could distribute Navigator by "carpet bombing"—mailing CD-ROM disks—or through downloading.

But Microsoft did not have to prohibit original equipment manufacturers from installing Netscape to ensure that most of them would not do so. Once IE became roughly equal in quality to Navigator, those manufacturers had no very good reason to ship two browsers and some reason—space on the desktop and disk, possible user confusion—not to do so. In fact, such shipments dropped sharply.

Similarly, Microsoft tied up the second major distribution channel by signing restrictive agreements with Internet service providers and online services that *explicitly* kept them from shipping "other browsers"—read "Navigator"—to more than a small fraction of their customers. Significantly, when, with the litigation about to begin, Microsoft waived such restrictions for many ISPs, it did not do so for the major online services: AOL, CompuServe, and Prodigy, nor for AT&T.

Of course, it remained true that Netscape was not cut off completely from customers. One exhibit sponsored by

Professor Schmalensee shows Navigator being delivered by parachutists. But "carpet bombing" is costly, and downloading of a complicated browser is ineffective. Consumers properly hesitate before undertaking such a task, particularly when a perfectly good browser already comes with their machine.[3]

In any event, it is browser *usage* that matters here, not browser opportunity or browser ownership or even browser installation. Microsoft's fear was that software applications writers would shift to writing for Navigator rather than for Windows and would thus weaken the applications barrier to entry into operating systems. That could happen if Navigator became very widely *used* relative to IE. It would not happen if Navigator was merely widely distributed or even widely installed and not used.

Significantly, the evidence as to the shift in share of browser *usage* is overwhelming. Evans and Schmalensee's claims to the contrary, Microsoft's attempt to dominate the browser market has been extremely successful. The AdKnowledge data used by the government at trial and described in chapter 1 clearly show that.[4] Indeed, one can see that by looking at a more recent source of hit data. According to Statmarket.com, which receives information from over 33 million Internet users visiting over 130,000 Web sites, IE's share of total browser usage reached 75.3 percent by August 2, 1999, and continued to grow to 79.4 percent on December 6, 1999. Microsoft has won the browser war.

Why, then, did AOL pay such a high price for Netscape? AOL bought a company with an Internet portal—and said so. The agreed-on price of $4 billion was in line with other such purchases. The browser wars were over, and the browser was not important in the purchase. As we pointed out in chapter 1, neither economic analysis nor the actions and statements of AOL suggest that AOL will abandon IE for Navigator. Even if it were someday to do so, the harm has already been done.

Evans and Schmalensee's chapter, like Professor Schmalensee's testimony, is replete with warnings about the wolf that might come out of the forest and end Microsoft's monopoly. Such possibilities are not excuses for antitrust violations designed to prevent such a thing from happening.

The Use of Intent Evidence

The government made much use of Microsoft's own statements. Evans and Schmalensee criticize such use, quoting at length from Fisher's book on the *IBM* case[5] on the dangers of relying on intent evidence. That quotation begins (emphasis added):

> The subjective intent of a company is difficult to determine and will *usually* reflect nothing more than a determination to win all possible business from rivals—a determination consistent with competition.

The operative word is *usually*. The quoted passage was written in the light of the *IBM* case, where the "usual" circumstance applied. The overwhelming flood of statements from Microsoft's executives and other employees[6] does not leave much ambiguity as to what was happening in this case.

Moreover, intent evidence can play a valuable role in a different way. Where the defendant claims to have taken its actions for other, procompetitive ends, clear, contemporaneous statements about intent can assist in evaluating that claim.

Little of the intent evidence in *Microsoft* can be confused with the intent of competing hard. Internal documents from Microsoft instead confirmed over and over the key elements of the government's case: that Microsoft did not believe that it could win the browser war by competing on the merits; that Windows was a powerful monopoly that could be used to compel cooperation in anticompetitive schemes; that the "bolting" of IE to Windows was designed to prevent competition, not serve consumers; and so on. The flood of internal memoranda and e-mails shows that Microsoft repeatedly took actions that made no business sense except as a means of disadvantaging rivals and thereby eliminating potential threats to Microsoft's monopoly position. The Pollyanna version of events invented for Microsoft's defense at trial with its vast public relations spin machine—a version still insisted upon by Evans and Schmalensee—is, at best, laughably naïve.

Innovation, the Antitrust Laws, and Microsoft's Attitude

As of this writing, indeed, it seems that the only lesson that Microsoft has learned from the case is that it should be cautious with its e-mails.[7] Before, during, and after the trial, Microsoft has mounted a consistent public relations campaign claiming that it is being persecuted because it is innovative and that antitrust policy is somehow inapplicable to an innovative firm or industry. Having had that claim rejected by the district court after an exhaustive multimonth trial, Microsoft now continues to pursue it and has gone so far as to lobby Congress to cut the budget of the Antitrust Division.

Evans and Schmalensee, doubtless out of conviction, have joined that campaign, referring to "an antiquated antitrust tool kit" and wishing to reargue all the facts as well as the findings of the court.

But the "antitrust tool kit" is not "antiquated." Indeed, and to the contrary, the Antitrust Division has used modern antitrust tools to analyze a range of competition issues in which innovation played a significant role.[8] Further, the fact that a firm is innovative does not give it a license to engage in anticompetitive activities designed to preserve monopoly power. Innovation, to be sure, may make it harder to decide when acts are anticompetitive, but it does not excuse them. Microsoft was not sued because of its innovations. Even the integration of the browser was not, taken alone, necessarily anticompetitive, although refusing to sell Windows and IE separately surely was.

It is fundamental and not at issue in this case that antitrust is not intended to protect *competitors,* but rather to protect *competition* in an industry as a whole. Thus, the issue is not Microsoft's innovations, which were legal and to be encouraged—when it is genuine innovation and not "bolting"—but rather overall, industrywide innovation. What society deserves is a high rate of industrywide innovation, following, if competition determines this, a variety of distinct paths that offer consumers real choice. Microsoft's anticompetitive acts worked to deny consumers such choices, first, by attacking specific innovations that showed the bad judgment to be made outside their company, and, second, by forcing the industrywide innovation path to adhere to a Windows-centric model.

Nor is the fact that a firm is innovative a reason to exempt it from antitrust scrutiny and liability. If that were the case, then firms would have every incentive to cloak their anticompetitive acts in a mantle—and mantra—of innovation. Despite the fact that the presumption that competition leads to consumer benefits comes from static propositions, a rule of law that protected attacks on competition in innovative industries would be an invitation to predation.

To paraphrase the words of Ernestine, Lily Tomlin's telephone operator, Microsoft's attitude to the entire antitrust process has been "We are Microsoft. We are innovative. *We are om-ni-po-tent.*" Fortunately for the rest of us, they are not.

4

Consumers Lose If Leading Firms Are Smashed for Competing

David S. Evans and Richard L. Schmalensee

It will be a sorry day for consumers—and the antitrust laws—if the courts choose to shatter one of the crown jewels of the U.S. economy on the dubious case presented by the government and summarized by Professors Fisher and Rubinfeld in chapter 1.[1]

They offer no evidence that Microsoft's behavior harms consumers and simply cite the court's speculations to that effect. Indeed, Fisher and Rubinfeld claim that proof of consumer harm really is not needed in predation cases, for consumers always benefit from low prices during predation. The harm comes later, they say, after competition has been eliminated.

That might be relevant if Microsoft's alleged predation had eliminated a competitor or was likely to do so. But Netscape, the alleged victim, is a division of America Online—one that continues to introduce innovative browsing software and to capture about a third of new browser users. AOL could have replaced Microsoft's Internet Explorer with Navigator as its preferred browser in January

1999; if it had done so, Netscape would have had roughly 60 percent of browser users. And, once again in January 2001, AOL will have the option to replace IE with its house-brand browser, a move that would add millions of users virtually overnight.

By the same token, Sun's Java is alive and well, with Java runtime environments present on almost all personal computers, including tens of millions of Windows 98 PCs. The most Fisher and Rubinfeld can claim is that Microsoft slowed Java down. But they write as if that amounted to murder.

Fisher and Rubinfeld round out their discussion of consumer harm with the court's conclusion that "Microsoft deters investment in technologies and businesses that exhibit the potential to threaten Microsoft."[2] But *any* response by Microsoft to competitive challenges, no matter how beneficial to consumers, would make potential competitors think twice. To condemn that sort of deterrence is to condemn competition. In any case, it is hard to imagine a market offering *less* evidence of investment deterred: Netscape's founders are now very rich; Sun is riding high; and firms marketing Linux or developing Web-based applications have become magnets for capital.

Nor do Fisher and Rubinfeld provide hard evidence that Microsoft's "bad acts" had any material effect—and indeed the court found virtually none. They contend that Microsoft asked Netscape to divide up markets, but, of course, Netscape turned that request down. They contend that Microsoft tried to force Apple to jettison QuickTime for Windows but omit the punch line: Apple said no.[3] Ditto for Microsoft's alleged attempts to strong-arm IBM and RealNetworks into staying clear of Windows' turf.[4]

Fisher and Rubinfeld contend that Microsoft forced Netscape to use costly channels of distribution. Yet AOL's investment bankers made no note of that difficulty in advising AOL that Netscape was worth billions of dollars. Indeed, they described Netscape's success in distributing its browser software.[5]

Stripped to basics, the government's case is about competing hard and being mean to rivals. The government offered bellicose snippets culled from millions of pages of Microsoft documents along with second- and third-hand reports of Microsoft executives making threatening statements at meetings.[6] And the government found lots of evidence that Microsoft was scared that Netscape, Sun, and others would grab some of its platform business—along with evidence that Microsoft competed very hard to stop them.

But the government did not come close to showing that Microsoft's actions have harmed consumers or ever would. And it is simply not illegal for a firm to compete hard to defend a leading market position.

Microsoft's decades-old strategy of licensing its operating systems widely, charging low prices, and investing in rapid innovation has played a major role in the PC revolution. That, in turn, has led to the Internet revolution—a revolution hastened by Microsoft's decision to drive the pace of innovation in browsing software. Microsoft discovered long ago that it could make a lot of money by giving consumers ever better features at low prices, and it applied that strategy aggressively to the Internet.

The core of the government's complaint is that Microsoft added "free" features to its operating system. But Microsoft has been adding features to its operating system in that way since it introduced MS-DOS 1.1 in 1982. To halt that behavior, which plainly benefits consumers, the government apparently wants to impose the antitrust equivalent of going nuclear—breaking Microsoft into several companies.

Prohibiting Successful Firms from Competing

According to Fisher and Rubinfeld—and the government—Microsoft's decision to improve Windows by adding browsing functionality was "a predatory anticompetitive act" because it involved "a deliberate sacrifice of profit to secure or protect monopoly power" (p. 9). Thus, a firm that has become very successful (read "has monopoly power") cannot aim to remain successful (read "protect monopoly power") by improving its products if it fails to charge extra for the improvements (read "sacrifices profits"). The application of that novel principle would be the death knell for competition in "winner-take-most" businesses like software, where firms fight to become and remain the market leader, for in such industries, product improvement by the leading firm will generally turn out to have been profitable only if it helps that leader to stay on top.

Tying and "Free" Browsers. Fisher and Rubinfeld conclude (p. 3) that adding browsing features to Windows without charging separately was anticompetitive—a remarkable conclusion since every other major provider of operating systems now includes browsing with no separate charge and since the main competitor to Windows in 1994 and 1995 (IBM's OS/2) added a "free" browser well before Microsoft did. An operating system that was not Internet-ready would be at a huge competitive disadvantage in today's Internet-focused market. Only by ignoring the real world can Fisher and Rubinfeld claim that no procompetitive reasons exist for adding browsing features to Windows.[7]

It is also remarkable that a lawsuit filed in May 1998 could challenge software design decisions made in 1994, especially when it is uncontested that the alleged victim of those decisions (Netscape) learned about them in 1994. Fisher and Rubinfeld contend that courts should compare consumer benefits from design decisions with their anticompetitive effects to decide on legality, although, as they note, the D.C. Court of Appeals has rejected that unworkable test in the present context. How could a software leader *ever* know whether it was legal to add a new feature to its product? The application of the standards advanced

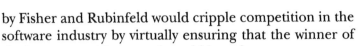

by Fisher and Rubinfeld would cripple competition in the software industry by virtually ensuring that the winner of the last competitive round would lose the next.

Fisher and Rubinfeld give two reasons why Microsoft's inclusion of browsing features was anticompetitive and should be condemned. First, they claim that Microsoft's browsing software, which they admit provides platform services, is a separate product from the Windows platform, which they admit also provides platform services. They accomplish that sleight of hand by casting Windows as solely an operating system, thereby obscuring the fact that browsing functionality is a natural part of a modern software platform.

Fisher and Rubinfeld are aware that since the release of IE 3.0, most of the software that provides browsing functionality in Windows also performs other essential system services. As Fisher and Rubinfeld know, the software that supports browsing thus cannot be removed without making Windows inoperative. Nonetheless, Fisher and Rubinfeld claim that Windows has a separate product called a browser. And they do so by repeatedly conflating the removal of the Windows "browser" with blocking access to Windows' browsing functionality.

Second, Fisher and Rubinfeld claim that adding "free" browsing to Windows sacrifices profits and therefore must be anticompetitive. But Microsoft has profited handsomely for its entire history by adding features to its operating systems at no separate charge. How could Microsoft have known that it was now obliged to offer crippled versions of its operating systems with fewer features or to charge extra for some new features? How could such policies, which no other popular operating system vendor follows, possibly benefit consumers? Yet that is where Fisher and Rubinfeld's novel test for anticompetitive behavior leads.

Fisher and Rubinfeld say that Microsoft sacrificed profits because it made browsing "free" in Windows. But to claim that one or another feature of Windows is free is absurd, since Windows is sold for a positive price. How can Fisher and Rubinfeld logically single out one particular feature in Windows as the offending freebie?

Fisher and Rubinfeld also argue that it made "no business sense" for Microsoft to give away browsing software for other operating systems, so predation is the only explanation for such behavior. In the real world, of course, *many* firms give away free software. For years, Apple has written versions of its QuickTime software for Windows and given it away. Competitive firms often do that to build usage and thus to obtain influence on the evolution of technical standards. Here, Microsoft was plainly unwilling to cede control of Internet standards to Netscape, and consumers are better off for that decision because those standards are now open.

Excluding Netscape from Distribution. Whether tagged as a "tie" or not, Microsoft's inclusion of browsing features in Windows did not foreclose Netscape from distribution. Nor did the contracts that the government and Fisher and Rubinfeld complain about. Microsoft's agreements with OEMs did not bar them from putting Navigator on the desktop. Netscape could and did enter into agreements with OEMs to include its browsing software on new computers. Consumers could and did install Navigator on Windows machines, just as they installed many other applications. Nor did the agreements with Internet access and content providers prevent Netscape from getting its software to consumers.

The Goldman Sachs due-diligence documents prepared for AOL on the eve of AOL's acquisition of Netscape, which both Fisher and Rubinfeld and the court assiduously ignore, make that absolutely clear. They say that Netscape distributed 160 million copies of Navigator to consumers in 1998 alone and had agreements with OEMs accounting for 22 percent of industry shipments despite "minimal promotion." They do *not* say that Netscape's ability to distribute its browsing software was hampered by anything other than weak marketing.[8] Perhaps most important, Netscape had no limitations on getting its browser into the hands of corporations, universities, and other institutions. The distribution channels Fisher and Rubinfeld cite are essentially irrelevant to that segment of the market, which accounts for almost half the sales of new PCs.

Netscape's problem was not distribution; it was getting people to *use* Navigator. But that is a symptom of competition, not monopoly. Microsoft serves consumers and obeys the law when it distributes a better browser that consumers choose to use. Fisher and Rubinfeld cannot deny that IE improved more rapidly than Navigator and is now generally recognized as superior.

Microsoft did distribute its browsing software aggressively. But it did so after Netscape had gained a very large share of what the government alleges is the "market for browsers" through innovation, coupled with widespread distribution of free software. Microsoft entered that "market" almost a year later and still had less than 10 percent of users when it signed the contracts the government complains are restrictive. No antitrust principle protects Jim Barksdale's "God-given right to a 95 percent market share" because Netscape was a trendy Internet start-up and Microsoft was a tough old software giant.

The most conclusive evidence of the importance of improved quality in driving up IE's market share comes from the portion of the market that did *not* connect to the Internet through AOL and other online services. Among those consumers, Microsoft's share did not start to grow rapidly until late 1997—long after the "bad" contracts took effect, but just after the widely praised IE 4 came out. Moreover, Microsoft's share among those users continued to rise after April 1998, when Microsoft waived restrictive contractual provisions on Internet service and content providers and gave computer makers more flexibility.

Muddying the Facts

Fisher and Rubinfeld dismiss the demonstration that the price of Windows predicted by the government's economic theory is many times higher than the actual price by asserting that the analysis had unspecified "material errors." In fact, it was the Justice Department's economist, Professor Fisher, who had to admit that his calculation of the predicted Windows price was in error because he used a price for personal computer systems that was too low by almost half. And it was he who used an absurdly high estimate for the elasticity of demand for personal computer systems—an elasticity implying that a 10 percent increase in price would cut sales by 40 percent.[9]

Fisher and Rubinfeld do not estimate a profit-maximizing price for Windows. At trial, Professor Fisher asserted that under "reasonable"—but unspecified—assumptions, the short-run profit-maximizing price of Windows was "within a couple hundred dollars" of the actual price in 1996 and 1997.[10] But getting within $200 of a price that is less than $65 would still mean a monopoly price four times higher than what Microsoft charges. The implied sacrifice of many billions in annual profits points to an enormous discrepancy between reality and the government's theory.

The government's attack on the survey data that Microsoft commissioned and relied on to measure browser use offers another example of "proof" through deception. The court rejected those data, in large part because the government argued that Microsoft did not use them in the ordinary course of business.[11] Professor Fisher claimed that when Microsoft executives said "usage" instead of "use," they were relying on a different type of data.[12] But in many of the "usage" e-mails, the Microsoft executives were indisputably discussing estimates based on the monthly surveys, which Microsoft has funded since early 1996, as the government knew from pretrial discovery. Moreover, the government and the court frequently cite other e-mails and internal presentations concerning how users got their browsers, all of which communications were based on the supposedly unreliable surveys. As a result, the government and its witness had it both ways. They implicitly used the surveys when it suited their purposes while they rejected systematic analysis of the same data because that analysis refuted many of their claims.

Is There an Applications Barrier to Entry?

The government contends that Microsoft is protected by an insurmountable applications barrier to entry. But Fisher and Rubinfeld do not explain why Navigator and Java were uniquely poised to break the "vicious cycle" in which software developers write for the most popular platform and consumers buy the platform with the most applications.

They do suggest that Navigator and Java could succeed as platforms because Navigator was a popular application in its own right that offered its own applications programming interfaces as well as those of Java (pp. 14–15). But that does not solve their problem. According to their theory, software developers will not write to APIs unless they are exposed by the most popular platform. And to make the transition from a widely distributed application to a wildly popular platform clearly requires a set of APIs rich enough to support a wide variety of attractive applications.

But Java has yet to manage that technical feat, and Netscape has never come close. Moreover, even if Navigator or Java were widely distributed and exposed the requisite APIs, the government's theory implies that it could not attract applications writers unless it were already the most popular *platform*. That is much more than a quibble: if the impregnable applications barrier does not exist—as Microsoft's fear of Netscape and Java and its aggressive Windows pricing clearly suggest—Microsoft's short-run market power is vulnerable to competition from many sources. Then, neither Netscape nor Java poses unique threats to Windows, and predation is not rational.

The Potential Legacy of the *Microsoft* Case

Suppose that the courts, accepting the conduct standards the government advances, ultimately rule against Microsoft and impose the draconian relief apparently sought by the government. A company that has delivered rapidly improving, popular software at low prices for a quarter century will be broken up, and the pieces of what once was Microsoft will be forced to struggle to regain momentum—perhaps under tight regulation by the court.

And what will be the lesson for others? Leading software companies will have strong incentives to pull their competitive punches to avoid being condemned for spending money to defend their "monopolies." And they will be reluctant to integrate new features into existing software for fear that some economist, years after the fact, will persuade some judge that, on balance, the integration had been anticompetitive—all because Microsoft had the temerity to compete with Netscape and the nerve to be tough in negotiations.

Appendix

The following acronyms appear in this monograph:

ABE: applications barrier to entry

AOL: America Online

API: applications programming interface

ICP: Internet content provider

IE: Internet Explorer

ISP: Internet service provider

ISV: independent software vendor

JRE: Java Runtime Environment

JVM: Java Virtual Machine

MSN: Microsoft Network

NSP: Native Signal Processing

OEM: original equipment manufacturer

OLS: online service

OS: operating system

Notes

Chapter 1: *United States* v. *Microsoft:*
An Economic Analysis

1. *United States* v. *Microsoft,* Civil Action No. 98-1232.

2. We are grateful to Jeffrey Blattner, David Boies, Timothy Bresnahan, Wayne Dunham, Joen Greenwood, Karma Giullianelli, A. Douglas Melamed, Diane Owen, Mark Popovsky, Mary Beth Savio, and others for assistance and comments on our analysis. None of the views expressed herein necessarily reflects their opinions or those of the Department of Justice.

3. In general, it takes less to prevent Netscape's browser from evolving into an alternative platform than it does to monopolize the browser market. We do not discuss the latter issues in this analysis.

4. U.S. Department of Justice, *Merger Guidelines* § I (1982), reprinted in *Trade Regulation Reports* 4 (CCH) ¶ 13,102; U.S. Department of Justice and Federal Trade Commission, *Horizontal Merger Guidelines* § 1.0 (1992), reprinted in *Trade Regulation Reports* 4 (CCH) ¶ 13,104.

5. Note that this need not require a quantitative estimate of the competitive price level; in intellectual property, in particular, where marginal costs are close to zero, that level may be difficult to determine. Nevertheless, as was true in *Microsoft,* it may be easy to use the testimony of customers to decide that a firm has the power to raise price above already remunerative levels.

6. Network effects are broadly discussed in Michael L. Katz and Carl Shapiro, "Antitrust in Software Markets," in Jeffrey A. Eisenach and Thomas M. Lenard, eds., *Competition, Innovation, and the Microsoft Monopoly: Antitrust in the Digital Marketplace* (Washington, D.C.: Progress and Freedom Foundation, 1999).

7. For a broader discussion of the implications of network effects, see Daniel L. Rubinfeld, "Antitrust Enforcement in Dynamic Network Industries," *Antitrust Bulletin* (Winter 1998): 859–82.

8. The second part of the definition is useful to distinguish a predatory anticompetitive act from one that merely turns out to lose money ex post.

9. The expected profits would necessarily take into account uncertain future streams of income, such as the payoffs from research and development.

10. The standard tests of predatory anticompetitive acts are not conceptually at odds with this definition. Areeda and Turner, for example, propose a test for a single-product firm in terms of price and average variable cost, but as long as the measure of cost reflects opportunity cost, the test becomes an important application of the general principle. See Phillip E. Areeda and Donald F. Turner, "Predatory Pricing and Related Practices under Section 2 of the Sherman Act," *Harvard Law Review* 88 (1975): 697–733. Furthermore, the Areeda-Turner article discusses predatory pricing, which is merely one type of predatory anticompetitive act.

11. In the court's findings of fact (hereafter CFOF), Judge Jackson agreed. He found that the relevant market is the licensing of all Intel-compatible PC operating systems worldwide (CFOF ¶ 18).

12. See, for example, John Romano, April 13, 1998, Deposition Transcript, p. 50 (Hewlett-Packard); Bart Brown, March 5, 1998, Deposition Transcript, pp. 10–11 (Gateway); James von Holle, September 19, 1997, Deposition Transcript, pp. 12–13 (Gateway); Jon Kies, April 23, 1998, Deposition Transcript, p. 8 (Packard Bell); Stephen Decker, October 17, 1997, Deposition Transcript, pp. 11–12 (Compaq).

13. See Government Exhibit 309.

14. See, for example, Plaintiff's Trial Exhibit 1.

15. On the applications barrier to entry, see, for example, Ron Rasmussen, July 10, 1998, Deposition Transcript, p. 67 (SCO); James von Holle, September 19, 1997, Deposition Transcript, p. 9 (Gateway); Frank Santos, April 13, 1998, Deposition Transcript, p. 9 (Hewlett-Packard); and Brad Chase, March 25, 1998, Deposition Transcript, p. 97 (Microsoft).

16. For example, Joachim Kempin, senior vice president of the OEM Sales Division at Microsoft, testified that he set the roy-

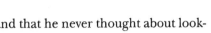

alty rates for Windows 98 and that he never thought about looking at other vendors (Joachim Kempin, March 18, 1998, Deposition Transcript, pp. 75–78).

17. See, for example, December 16, 1997, regarding "As promised OEM pricing thoughts," Joachim Kempin to Bill Gates et al.: Plaintiff's Trial Exhibit 365, p. MS7 007196.

18. Judge Jackson agreed. He stated: "Viewed together, three main facts indicate that Microsoft enjoys monopoly power. First, Microsoft's share of the market for Intel-compatible PC operating systems is extremely large and stable. Second, Microsoft's dominant market share is protected by a high barrier to entry. Third, and largely as a result of that barrier, Microsoft's customers lack a commercially viable alternative to Windows" (CFOF ¶ 34).

19. The court found that "the growth of server- and middleware-based applications development might eventually weaken the applications barrier to entry. . . . But, . . . it is not clear whether ISVs [independent software vendors] will ever develop a large, diverse body of full-featured applications that rely solely on APIs [applications programming interfaces] exposed by servers and middleware. Furthermore, even assuming that such a movement has already begun in earnest, it will take several years for the applications barrier to erode enough to enable a non-Microsoft, Intel-compatible PC operating system to develop into a viable alternative to Windows" (CFOF ¶ 56).

20. As early as May 1995, Ben Slivka, at that time a Microsoft project leader for Internet Explorer, noted, "My nightmare scenario is that the Web grows into a rich application platform in an operating system–neutral way" (May 27, 1995, "The Web Is the Next Platform (version 5)," Plaintiff's Trial Exhibit 21, pp. MS98 0102395–6). Similarly, in his FY97 Planning Memo, "Winning the Internet Platform Battle," Brad Chase of Microsoft wrote: "This is a no revenue product, but you should worry about your browser share, as much as Bill G because . . . we will lose the Internet platform battle if we do not have a significant user installed base" (April 4, 1996, "FY97 Planning Memo: 'Winning the Internet Platform Battle,'" Brad Chase to FY97 WWSMM Attendees: Plaintiff's Trial Exhibit 39, p. MS6 5005720). Similarly, in a slide presentation for the "IPTD Division Meeting," Brad Silverberg, then senior vice president of the Internet Platforms and Tools Division at Microsoft, wrote:"The Internet Battle: This

is not about browsers. Our competitors are trying to create an alternative *platform* to Windows®" (April 25, 1996, Plaintiff's Trial Exhibit 40, p. MS6 6005550).

The browser could also have threatened the operating system monopoly by providing an alternative user interface. As a result, browsers could have reduced consumers' resistance to non-Windows operating systems and enabled businesses to use different operating systems. In turn, that would have reduced Microsoft's power to exploit the value of its interface real estate by requiring other companies to promote Microsoft's products through exclusive agreements (Brad Chase, March 25, 1998, Deposition Transcript, p. 39). Microsoft was also concerned that browsers could develop into an alternative software development platform that could replace Windows (Bill Gates, April 10, 1996, "The Internet PC," Plaintiff's Trial Exhibit 336, p. MS7 007443; Benjamin Slivka, September 3, 1998, Deposition Transcript, pp. 252–53; James Allchin, March 19, 1998, Deposition Transcript, p. 116).

21. June 20, 1996, regarding "windows & internet issues," Paul Maritz to Brad Silverberg et al.: Plaintiff's Trial Exhibit 42, pp. MS6 6010346–47; April 21, 1997, Brad Chase to Jeff Raikes et al.: Plaintiff's Trial Exhibit 59, p. MS7 004365.

22. May 26, 1995, Bill Gates to executive staff and direct reports regarding "The Internet Tidal Wave": Plaintiff's Trial Exhibit 20, p. MS98 0112876.3. That would have ensured that, for the foreseeable future, Microsoft would produce the only platform-level browsing software distributed to run on Windows. That would have eliminated the prospect that non-Microsoft browsing software could weaken the applications barrier to entry.

23. According to the court, "Microsoft's first response to the threat posed by Navigator was an effort to persuade Netscape to structure its business such that the company would not distribute platform-level browsing software for Windows." Netscape's assent would have ensured that, "for the foreseeable future, Microsoft would produce the only platform-level browsing software distributed to run on Windows. This would have eliminated the prospect that non-Microsoft browsing software could weaken the applications barrier to entry" (CFOF ¶ 78).

See the testimony of the participants in the June 1995 meetings and contemporaneous documents (for example, Barksdale Transcript, p. 236; Marc Andreessen, July 15, 1998, Deposition

Transcript, pp. 463–72). For evidence that Microsoft made an effort to induce Netscape to agree to draw a line between Windows 95 browsers and other browser-related products, see June 21, 1995, Marc Andreessen to jimb et al.: Plaintiff's Trial Exhibit 547, p. NET 000914; Plaintiff's Trial Exhibit 33, p. NSC017098; June 1, 1995, regarding "working with Netscape," Thomas Reardon to Ben Slivka, Paul Maritz, et al.: Plaintiff's Trial Exhibit 24, p. MS98 0009597.

24. July 8, 1996, Brent Schlender, "A Conversation with the Lords of Wintel," *Fortune:* Plaintiff's Trial Exhibit 559, p. 8.

25. May 25, 1995, Gates to Grove: Plaintiff's Trial Exhibit 277, p. MS98 1069352. According to Mr. Gates: "The main problem between us right now is NSP [Native Signal Processing]. We are trying to convince them to basically not ship NSP." (July 7, 1995, regarding "Our Dinner," Gates to Silverberg et al.: Plaintiff's Trial Exhibit 278, p. MS98 0169009). Mr. Gates also reported: "Andy believes Intel is living up to its part of the NSP bargain and that we should let OEMs [original equipment manufacturers] know that some of the new software work Intel is doing is OK" (Plaintiff's Trial Exhibit 381).

26. Judge Jackson found: "[T]he software threatened to offer ISVs [independent software vendors] and device manufacturers an alternative to waiting for Windows to provide system-level support for products that would take advantage of advances in hardware technology. More troubling was the fact that Intel was developing versions of its NSP [Native Signal Processing] software for non-Microsoft operating systems. The different versions of the NSP software exposed the same set of software interfaces to developers, so the more an application took advantage of interfaces exposed by NSP software, the easier it would be to port that application to non-Microsoft operating systems. In short, Intel's NSP software bore the potential to weaken the barrier protecting Microsoft's monopoly power" (CFOF ¶ 97).

27. Steven McGeady, August 10, 1998, Deposition Transcript, pp. 11–12, 18–20, 34–37, 57–60, 64–67; "On August 2, 1995, in a meeting of Intel and Microsoft executives, Bill Gates told Intel CEO Andy Grove to shut down the Intel Architecture Labs. Gates didn't want IAL's 750 engineers interfering with his plans for domination of the PC industry" (August 28, 1995, Plaintiff's Trial Exhibit 280, p. INT 0386).

28. June 9, 1996, Gates to Maritz et al.: Plaintiff's Trial Exhibit 289, p. MS98 0169187.

29. For example, Microsoft's general manager for Internet multimedia, Eric Engstrom, wrote to his superiors that he was working "aggressively" to convince "Intel to stop helping Sun create Java Multimedia APIs [applications programming interfaces], especially ones that run well (i.e. native implementations) on Windows" (May 26, 1997, Eric Engstrom to John Ludwig and David Cole et al.: Plaintiff's Trial Exhibit 235, p. MS7 027416).

30. Timothy Schaaff, August 28, 1998, Deposition Transcript, pp. 37–38.

31. Schaaff, August 28, 1998, Deposition Transcript, p. 42.

32. Schaaff, August 28, 1998, Deposition Transcript, pp. 38–41, 60.

33. With respect to QuickTime, Judge Jackson commented that "the primary motivation behind Microsoft's proposal to Apple was not the resolution of incompatibilities that frustrated consumers and stymied content development. Rather, Microsoft's motivation was its desire to limit as much as possible the development of multimedia content that would run cross-platform" (CFOF ¶ 110).

34. Direct Testimony of Richard L. Schmalensee ¶ 211; Mehdi Deposition, January 13, 1999, p. 655: 4–20 (the IE fiscal year 1997 marketing budget was roughly $30 million).

35. July 24, 1996, regarding "Intuit call with Scott Cook," Bill Gates to Lewis Levin et al.: Plaintiff's Trial Exhibit 94, p. MS6 6007642.

36. April 4, 1996, regarding "FY97 Planning Memo: 'Winning the Internet Platform Battle'"; Brad Chase to FY97 WWSMM Attendees: Plaintiff's Trial Exhibit 39, p. M6 5005720.

37. Bill Gates, August 27, 1998, Deposition Transcript, p. 236.

38. Steven McGeady, August 10, 1998, Deposition Transcript, pp. 16–17.

39. In its defense, Microsoft argued that it needed to offer IE to Apple so that enterprises that had an installed Mac base and wanted to standardize on a single browser would find Windows 98 attractive for users who were not part of the Mac base or were willing to switch operating systems.

40. Government Exhibit 39.

41. Silverberg Deposition, January 13, 1999, pp. 703: 13–705: 11.

42. The price is negative because Microsoft gives up valuable concessions such as space on the desktop (and the opportunity

to earn money therefrom) in exchange for commitments to distribute its browser. See Plaintiff's Trial Exhibit 1115 (Internet service provider referral fees).

43. Judge Jackson found: "[H]ad Microsoft not viewed browser usage share as the key to preserving the applications barrier to entry, the company would not have taken its efforts beyond developing a competitive browser product, including it with Windows at no additional cost to consumers, and promoting it with advertising. . . . [T]he considerable additional cost[] associated with enlisting other firms in its campaign to increase Internet Explorer's usage share at Navigator's expense . . . was only profitable to the extent that it protected the applications barrier to entry. . . . Microsoft's costly efforts to limit the use of Navigator on Windows could not have stemmed from a desire to bolster consumer demand for Windows" (CFOF ¶ 141).

44. See Steven C. Salop and David T. Scheffman, "Cost-Raising Strategies," *Journal of Industrial Economics* 36 (1987): 19–34.

45. August 8, 1997, regarding "post-agreement," Bill Gates to Paul Maritz et al.: Plaintiff's Trial Exhibit 265.

46. In the traditional terminology of economics, bundling relates to situations in which firms sell packages of two or more products. *Tying*, often used interchangeably with *bundling*, is applied by many economists to cases in which the consumer must purchase one product to obtain another. With that terminology, it is appropriate in our view to describe the browser as having been bundled with and tied to the operating system.

47. The court found, "Many consumers desire to separate their choice of a Web browser from their choice of an operating system" (CFOF ¶ 151). "Moreover, many consumers who need an operating system, including a substantial percentage of corporate consumers, do not want a browser at all" (CFOF ¶ 152).

48. January 2, 1997, "IE and Windows," J. Allchin to Paul Maritz: Plaintiff's Trial Exhibit 48; February 24, 1997, C. Wildfeuer to Adam Taylor et al.: Plaintiff's Trial Exhibit 202, p. MS7 004346.

49. The court found: "When a user chooses a browser other than Internet Explorer as the default, Windows 98 nevertheless requires the user to employ Internet Explorer in numerous situations that, from the user's perspective, are entirely unexpected. As a consequence, users who choose a browser other than Internet Explorer as their default face considerable uncertainty and confusion in the ordinary course of using Windows 98" (CFOF ¶ 171).

Further, the court held: "The decision to override the user's selection of non-Microsoft software as the default browser also directly disinclined Windows 98 consumers to use Navigator as their default browser, and it harmed those Windows 98 consumers who nevertheless used Navigator. In particular, Microsoft exposed those using Navigator on Windows 98 to security and privacy risks that are specific to Internet Explorer and to ActiveX controls" (CFOF ¶ 172).

50. Judge Jackson asserted: "Microsoft's actions have inflicted collateral harm on consumers who have no interest in using a Web browser at all. If these consumers want the nonbrowsing features available only in Windows 98, they must content themselves with an operating system that runs more slowly than if Microsoft had not interspersed browsing-specific routines throughout various files containing routines relied upon by the operating system. More generally, Microsoft has forced Windows 98 users uninterested in browsing to carry software that, while providing them with no benefits, brings with it . . . costs [that] . . . include performance degradation, increased risk of incompatibilities, and the introduction of bugs. Corporate consumers . . . who do not want Web browsing at all . . . are further burdened in that they are denied a simple and effective means of preventing employees from attempting to browse the Web" (CFOF ¶ 173). He also found: "Microsoft has harmed even those consumers who desire to use Internet Explorer, and no other browser, with Windows 98. To the extent that browsing-specific routines have been commingled with operating system routines to a greater degree than is necessary to provide any consumer benefit, Microsoft has unjustifiably . . . increased the likelihood that a browser crash will cause the entire system to crash and made it easier for malicious viruses that penetrate the system via Internet Explorer to infect non-browsing parts of the system" (CFOF ¶ 174).

51. Richard T. Brownrigg, March 5, 1998, Deposition Transcript, p. 34; Mal Ransom, March 19, 1998, Deposition Transcript, p. 28; Webb McKinney, March 13, 1998, Deposition Transcript, pp. 29–30.

52. Stephen Decker, October 17, 1997, Deposition Transcript, p. 22.

53. Judge Jackson concluded: "In sum, Microsoft successfully secured for Internet Explorer—and foreclosed to Navigator—

one of the two distribution channels that leads most efficiently to the usage of browsing software. Microsoft achieved this feat by using a complementary set of tactics. First, it forced OEMs [original equipment manufacturers] to take Internet Explorer with Windows and forbade them to remove or obscure it. . . . Second, Microsoft imposed additional technical restrictions to increase the cost of promoting Navigator even more. Third, Microsoft offered OEMs valuable consideration in exchange for commitments to promote Internet Explorer exclusively. Finally, Microsoft threatened to penalize individual OEMs that insisted on pre-installing and promoting Navigator. Although Microsoft's campaign to capture the OEM channel succeeded, it required a massive and multifarious investment by Microsoft; it also stifled innovation by OEMs that might have made Windows PC systems easier to use and more attractive to consumers. That Microsoft was willing to pay this price demonstrates that its decision-makers believed that maximizing Internet Explorer's usage share at Navigator's expense was worth almost any cost" (CFOF ¶ 241).

54. In early January 1999, Compaq announced the installation of Navigator on the desktop of some of its machines. Significantly, Netscape had to pay Compaq several hundred thousand dollars for that. Microsoft had successfully raised the costs of its rival.

55. August 5, 1997, "Technology Agreement between Apple Computer, Inc., and Microsoft Corporation": Plaintiff's Trial Exhibit 1167, pp. MAC 0044–45.

56. Avadis Tevanian, July 17, 1998, Deposition Transcript, pp. 135–42. Judge Jackson concluded, "By extracting from Apple terms that significantly diminished the usage of Navigator on the Mac OS, Microsoft severely sabotaged Navigator's potential to weaken the applications barrier to entry" (CFOF ¶ 356).

57. Mr. Allchin agreed "that you can get those benefits [the browsing experience] either by buying Windows 98 or by having purchased an original retail version of Windows 95 to which you added IE 4 either downloaded or bought from retail or gotten in some other way." Allchin Testimony, February 1, 1999, P.M. Session Transcript, p. 45: 9–25.

58. See, for example, Felton, January 14, 1998, A.M. Session Transcript, pp. 60: 18–61: 2.

59. *United States* v. *Microsoft Corporation*, 147 F.3d 935 (D.C. Circuit 1998).

60. Professor Felten explained: "It is possible to construct a mechanism for removing Web browsing from Windows 98. . . . This demonstrates that Microsoft could have produced a version of Windows 98 without Web browsing in a way that did not endanger the functionality of the operating system" (Edward W. Felten, September 1, 1998, Expert Report, pp. 13–14). Importantly, the court found, "No consumer benefit can be ascribed, however, to Microsoft's refusal to offer a version of Windows 95 or Windows 98 without Internet Explorer, or to Microsoft's refusal to provide a method for uninstalling Internet Explorer from Windows 98" (CFOF ¶ 186).

61. Carl Bass, November 21, 1997, Declaration ¶¶ 4–6; John Gailey, November 17, 1997, Declaration ¶ 4.

62. Brad Silverberg, April 14, 1998, Deposition Transcript, p. 159.

63. Michael A. Cusumano and David B. Yoffie, *Competing on Internet Time: Lessons from Netscape and Its Battle with Microsoft* (New York: Simon & Schuster, 1998), p. 112; Brad Silverberg, April 14, 1998, Deposition Transcript, p. 187.

64. Even when a customer specifically requested another browser, the Internet service provider could not provide another browser if doing so would cause the total shipments of its non-Microsoft browsers to exceed a specified percentage, typically 25 percent, of all browsers shipped by that provider.

65. Cameron Myhrvold, August 7, 1998, Declaration ¶ 4; April 21, 1998, Cameron Myhrvold of Microsoft to Leland C. Thoburn: Plaintiff's Trial Exhibit 374, pp. MS98 0106631–32.

66. July 14, 1997, regarding "(not so) random marketing thoughts," Paul Maritz to Moshe Dunie, Bill Gates, et al.: Plaintiff's Trial Exhibit 113, p. MS7 027366; January 5, 1997, regarding "overview slides for Billg/NC&Java session with 14+'s on Monday," Paul Maritz to Bill Gates, Jim Allchin, Ben Slivka, and Brad Silverberg: Plaintiff's Trial Exhibit 51, pp. MS7 005534, 005536.

67. "VJ98 SKUs and Pricing-Proposal": Plaintiff's Trial Exhibit 259, p. MS7 033448.

68. James Gosling, September 10, 1998, Declaration ¶ 16.

69. March 27, 1997, regarding "ie data," Kumar Mehta to Brad Chase et al.: Plaintiff's Trial Exhibit 204.

70. May 19, 1996, regarding "Some Thoughts on Netscape," Bill Gates to Paul Maritz et al.: Plaintiff's Trial Exhibit 41, p. MS6 6012952.

71. "Netscape Competitive Analysis": Plaintiff's Trial Exhibit 835, pp. MS98 0112834–36.

72. Plaintiff's Trial Exhibit 12.

73. March 27, 1997, regarding "ie data," Kumar Mehta to Brad Chase et al.: Plaintiff's Trial Exhibit 204.

74. Homer Transcript 70.

75. See Plaintiff's Trial Exhibit 11.

76. For example, not every Internet service provider can be readily individually identified in the AdKnowledge data. The domain names, and thus the data for some of the providers, could not be found. Further, hits by AOL subscribers are underrepresented because of AOL's use of "caching," a device that makes repeated "hits" on a given page by the same or different AOL subscribers occur through AOL's own server rather than in a manner measured by AdKnowledge. In the way in which we have used the data, that phenomenon leads to an understatement of the effects of Microsoft's restrictive practices.

77. Judge Jackson distinguished three categories of Internet access providers (IAPs): "One category was hits originating from subscribers to IAPs that, according to a chart prepared by Microsoft for its internal use, were not subject to any distribution or promotion restrictions. Another category was hits originating from subscribers to any IAP. A third category was hits originating from subscribers to AOL and CompuServe. . . . The differences in the degree of Internet Explorer's success in the three categories reveal the exclusionary effect of Microsoft's interdiction of Navigator in the IAP channel" (CFOF ¶ 310).

78. For example, on February 6, 1998, Microsoft estimated that its share of the browser market had increased from 6 percent in June 1996, to 31 percent in June 1997, to 40 percent in December 1997, and to 45 percent in January 1998 and projected that Microsoft's share would increase to 57 percent in June 1999, to 61 percent in June 2000, and to 65 percent in June 2001 (February 6, 1998, Haas to Chase et al.: Plaintiff's Trial Exhibit 310 and Plaintiff's Trial Exhibit 14). Further, data from AdKnowledge show Microsoft's share of browser usage increasing from 20 percent in January 1997 to 49 percent in August 1998. Microsoft's incremental share (the change in IE users divided by the change in total users) was even higher. Microsoft estimated that its incremental

share of users for the last six months of 1997 was 57 percent (Plaintiff's Trial Exhibit 8).

79. See Plaintiff's Trial Exhibits 6 and 7.

80. The court found: "Microsoft's efforts to maximize Internet Explorer's share of browser usage at Navigator's expense have done just that. The period since 1996 has witnessed a large increase in the usage of Microsoft's browsing technologies and a concomitant decline in Navigator's share. This reversal of fortune might not have occurred had Microsoft not improved the quality of Internet Explorer, and some part of the reversal is undoubtedly attributable to Microsoft's decision to distribute Internet Explorer with Windows at no additional charge. The relative shares would not have changed nearly as much as they did, however, had Microsoft not devoted its monopoly power and monopoly profits to precisely that end" (CFOF ¶ 358).

81. Our conclusion follows not simply from the fact that consumer choices were reduced, since as a conceptual matter, some product changes or marketing practices may harm some consumers while benefiting others. Rather, we believe that Microsoft's conduct would not have been undertaken (because it was not otherwise profitable), but for the exclusion of competitors and the opportunity to recoup by maintaining and increasing monopoly power in its operating system.

82. CFOF ¶ 409.

83. CFOF ¶ 410.

84. CFOF ¶ 411.

85. CFOF ¶ 412.

Chapter 2: How the Government Is Selling an Antitrust Case

1. *United States of America* v. *Microsoft Corporation,* Civil Action No. 98-1232 (TPJ), and *State of New York et al.* v. *Microsoft Corporation,* Civil Action No. 98-1233 (TPJ) (hereafter *United States* v. *Microsoft*). For brevity, "the government" refers to "the U.S. Department of Justice and nineteen states" that were coplaintiffs. Three economists testified at trial: Professor Franklin Fisher for the Justice Department, Dr. Frederick Warren-Boulton for the state coplaintiffs, and Dean Richard Schmalensee for Microsoft.

2. The complaint was filed in May 1998, and trial testimony concluded in June 1999. The court issued its formal findings of fact in November 1999 and accepted most of the government's arguments. The parties completed their briefings on the next formal stage of the trial, the conclusions of law, in January 2000. Unless the parties settle or the case is dropped, the court will then issue its conclusions of law and, if adverse to Microsoft, consider remedies. Either party may appeal the court's final judgment to the Court of Appeals for the D.C. Circuit. See http://www.neramicrosoft.com/level_1/nera_tt.htm for the legal documents cited in this analysis. We are indebted to Albert Nichols for helpful comments.

3. See the court's findings of fact in *United States* v. *Microsoft,* November 5, 1999 (hereafter CFOF).

4. CFOF ¶ 408.

5. CFOF ¶ 411.

6. No evidence cited by the court or in the trial record shows that a substantial number of consumers wanted a browserless copy of Windows. See CFOF ¶¶ 409–10.

7. CFOF ¶ 410.

8. CFOF ¶ 411.

9. Direct Testimony of James Allchin in *United States* v. *Microsoft* (hereafter Allchin Direct) ¶¶ 215–35.

10. Direct Testimony of Richard L. Schmalensee in *United States* v. *Microsoft* (hereafter Schmalensee Direct) ¶ 212.

11. February 2, 1999, P.M. Session Transcript, pp. 51–52 (James Allchin).

12. Direct Testimony of Daniel Rosen in *United States* v. *Microsoft* ¶¶ 26–29; Defendant's Exhibit 742.

13. Michael A. Cusumano and David B. Yoffie, *Competing on Internet Time: Lessons from Netscape and Its Battle with Microsoft* (New York: Free Press, 1998), pp. 98–100. Excerpts from this book were submitted as a trial exhibit by the government (Plaintiff's Trial Exhibit 1372).

14. The versions of Internet Explorer developed and distributed for non-Windows platforms use different software code from the Windows version, though they implement the same standards. Moreover, all non-Windows versions of IE are applications programs and not integrated into the operating systems on which they run.

15. CFOF ¶ 89; plaintiff's proposed findings of fact (hereafter PPFOF) PPFOF ¶ 56.1; Direct Testimony of Paul Maritz in *United States* v. *Microsoft* (hereafter Maritz Direct) ¶ 113.

16. See Michael A. Cusumano and David B. Yoffie, *Competing on Internet Time: Lessons from Netscape and Its Battle with Microsoft* (New York: Free Press, 1998), p. 40.

17. Schmalensee Direct ¶ 137; "Sell-Out Crowd to Attend Netscape Internet Devcon This Week to See Latest Java and Javascript Tools," *PR Newswire*, March 4, 1996.

18. Defendant's proposed findings of fact in *United States v. Microsoft* ¶ 44.

19. Microsoft's Answers to Interrogatories in Civil Investigative Demand 18140, answer to Interrogatory 4.

20. Schmalensee Direct ¶¶ 255–60; Direct Testimony of Brad Chase in *United States v. Microsoft* ¶¶ 100–36; Defendant's Exhibits 11–33; Defendant's Exhibit 2355. Although the government presented no systematic evidence to the contrary, the court appears to have concluded that the IE 4 was only equal in quality to Navigator 4 (CFOF ¶ 135).

21. The first of those figures is based on a survey of browser use conducted monthly for Microsoft beginning in April 1996 and regularly used by Microsoft executives in the course of market analysis. The survey by Market Decisions Corporation (MDC) provided the only systematic evidence on how users obtained their browsers—evidence that was wholly at odds with the government's assertions about Netscape's foreclosure from some distribution channels. The judge ruled that the survey was unreliable (CFOF ¶ 371). He apparently relied on testimony by the Justice Department's economist, Professor Franklin Fisher, that some respondents gave inconsistent answers to two questions (CFOF ¶ 371), although Fisher did not attempt to show that excluding those respondents would affect any conclusions. The government relied on data collected, beginning in January 1997, to measure visits ("hits") to Web sites that carry advertising. Neither Netscape nor Microsoft used those data to measure browser shares. Although the government's data do not begin until 1997, other sources of "hit" data tend to show a higher share than survey data for Navigator before 1997 because of problems dealing with "hits" from subscribers of AOL and other online services. (The survey finds that online service subscribers generally used the browser their service supplied, while the hit data imply that they generally used Navigator.) Survey and hit data give very similar results for users who were not subscribers to online services. For

a more detailed discussion of those issues, see Schmalensee Direct, appendix D; Richard Schmalensee, "Rebuttal of Survey/Statistical Issues Concerning Foreclosure," June 17, 1999; and National Economic Research Associates, "Notes on Issues Concerning Shares of Browser Use" (Cambridge, Mass.: National Economic Research Associates, December 6, 1999).

22. See Kara Swisher, *aol.com* (New York: Random House, 1998), pp. 133–41.

23. CFOF ¶ 288.

24. CFOF ¶ 288.

25. Swisher, pp. 135–36.

26. NERA's calculations were based on MDC data. The government's browser data showed Netscape's share among AOL members to be close to 70 percent in early 1997. But that was totally inconsistent with all other sources of information, which showed that most AOL users have employed the default browser provided by the company. In early 1997, AOL had only recently switched to the IE-based software, so most of its subscribers still had the older Booklink browser. See Schmalensee Direct, appendix D, for a more detailed discussion of that and other browser data issues.

27. CFOF ¶ 248.

28. CFOF ¶ 250.

29. CFOF ¶¶ 264–65.

30. CFOF ¶ 268.

31. Removing that software from Windows 95/98 (involving IE 3 and later versions) would cripple the operating system, since much of it is employed by other parts of the operating system— for example, to display help files and directory information.

32. See generally Cusumano and Yoffie.

33. October 20, 1998, P.M. Session Transcript, pp. 72–73 (Barksdale).

34. See June 21, 1999, P.M. Session Transcript, p. 32 (Schmalensee); http://media.web.aol.com/media/press_view.cfm?release_num= 100069&title=AMERICA%20ONLINE%2C%20INC%2E%20 COMPLETES%20ACQUISITION%20OF%20NETSCAPE% 20COMMUNICATIONS%20CORPORATION.

35. Those estimates are based on the MDC data. The data used by the government show a much sharper drop in Netscape's share (Schmalensee Direct, appendix D ¶ 2) because, as noted above,

they do not properly measure the use of "other" browsers by online service providers in 1996 and early 1997 (ibid. ¶¶ 95–97).

36. June 3, 1999, A.M. Session Transcript, p. 60 (Fisher).

37. If we assume that Netscape's share equals its incremental share of 35 percent in 2001 and all of AOL's IE users switched to Netscape, Netscape's share would be 55 percent.

38. Most computer languages are compiled into machine code that can run only on a specific hardware-software platform. If a program is written generically, however, it is a simple matter to recompile it for different platforms. It is more time-consuming if substantial parts of the program must be modified before it can be recompiled for a different platform.

39. Larry Seltzer, "Editors' Choice: Microsoft JVM for Windows," *PC Magazine*, April 7, 1998.

40. CFOF ¶ 401.

41. Defendant's Exhibit 1952; Direct Testimony of Robert Muglia in *United States* v. *Microsoft* ¶ 129.

42. Lotus, for example, has discontinued support of *e-suite* (http://www.lotus.com/home.nsf/welcome/esuite1), which was written in Java, and Netscape abandoned efforts to write a new browser completely in Java (October 26, 1998, A.M. Session Transcript, pp. 34–35 (Barksdale)).

43. This is not to diminish the advantages that Netscape had in being widely distributed. But there is no apparent reason why wide distribution gave Netscape greater advantages than Linux (which benefited from the open-source code model), Apple (which had a base of 12,000 applications and was a highly regarded operating system), or IBM (which at the time had the world's largest software firm backing its OS/2 operating system).

44. As noted above, Microsoft also offers versions of IE for other platforms and distributes them for free. Microsoft argued that such a practice responded to the demands of large multiplatform firms and reflected the general desirability of having one's technologies used; the government argued that the practice made no business sense—although many other firms produce and distribute free software—and was evidence of predation. Sorting that out might help interpret Microsoft's actions but is not material for assessing the *effects* of those actions, since most people use Windows.

45. See June 21, 1999, P.M. Session Transcript, p. 60 (Schmalensee), and Defendant's Exhibit 2763.

46. Netscape's actual share in early 1996 was almost certainly well below 80 percent because all the online services were still using older browsing software. The hit data widely used by Netscape and others to track browser share, however, did not appropriately count those users and thus gave Netscape a higher share. Outside the online services, however, all data sources used in the trial agree that Netscape had a share well above 70 percent throughout 1996. Netscape clearly perceived itself as having a very high share, which it hoped to expand further. Jim Barksdale, for example, has been quoted as saying, "All I want is my God-given 90 percent market share." (James Barksdale, as quoted in Barbara Darrow, "James Barksdale," *Computer Reseller News*, November 17, 1997). Although Barksdale has asserted that his statements of that sort were jokes, there clearly was an expectation that Netscape would dominate the supply of browsers and thus be able to determine future Internet standards.

47. *United States* v. *E. I. du Pont de Nemours & Co.*, 351 U.S. at 391 (1956).

48. David S. Evans and Richard Schmalensee, "A Guide to the Antitrust Economics of Networks," *Antitrust* 10:2 (1996), pp. 36–40. On the second of those mechanisms, see Richard L. Schmalensee, "Product Differentiation Advantages of Pioneering Brands," *American Economic Review* 72 (1982): 349–65.

49. David S. Evans, Albert Nichols, and Bernard Reddy, "The Rise and Fall of Leaders in Personal Computer Software," December 1998, http://www.neramicrosoft.com/NeraDocuments/Analyses/rise_and_fall.pdf.

50. See Joseph Farrell and Garth Saloner, "Installed Base and Compatibility: Innovation, Product Preannouncements, and Predation," *American Economic Review* 76 (1986): 940.

51. CFOF ¶ 34. The court also mentioned stable market share as evidence of monopoly power. But economists and the courts generally agree that high market share alone does not establish monopoly power, and this court relies almost entirely on the existence of the applications barrier.

52. CFOF ¶¶ 36–50. Those statements are consistent with testimony of the government's economists, although they articulate

it somewhat differently. The government's economists did not offer any additional theoretical or factual support beyond what is listed here.

53. CFOF ¶¶ 46–47.

54. For example, see Jim Carlton, *Apple: The Inside Story of Intrigue, Egomania, and Business Blunders* (New York: Random House, 1997); Owen W. Linzmayer, *Apple Confidential: The Real Story of Apple Computer, Inc.* (San Francisco: No Starch Press, 1999).

55. Apple licensed its OS for several years in the 1990s—but well after Windows had become popular. In the mid-1980s, Bill Gates urged Apple to license the OS, presumably to increase the market for Microsoft's popular Macintosh applications. Carlton, *Apple: The Inside Story of Intrigue, Egomania, and Business Blunders,* pp. 47–53, 156–66.

56. Craig Zarley, "OS/2 vs. DOS: The Decision's on Hold; PCs at the Crossroads Supplement," *PC Week,* November 14, 1988, p. S17; Kathleen Doler, "Firms Pit Unix against OS/2 in Market Battle for Operating Systems," *PC Week,* May 17, 1988, p. 17; John Dvorak, "Is DOS Dead?" *PC Computing,* August 1988, p. 122.

57. See, for example, IBM's advertisement for OS/2 in *PC Magazine,* November 12, 1991, pp. 26–27.

58. Paul Carroll, *Big Blues: The Unmaking of IBM* (New York: Random House, 1994); Daniel Quinn Mills and G. Bruce Friesen, *Broken Promises: An Unconventional View of What Went Wrong at IBM* (Cambridge: Harvard Business School Press, 1996).

59. Rebuttal Testimony of Richard Schmalensee, June 23, 1999, P.M. Session Transcript, p. 48. Also see Maritz Direct ¶ 149.

60. More than 2,500 applications were listed on http://www.linuxapps.com as of December 1, 1999.

61. Over 1,000 new applications were written to the MacOS within months of Apple's announcement of the iMac. See Defendant's Exhibit 1884 and cross-examination of Warren-Boulton on November 23, 1998, P.M. Session Transcript, pp. 17–19.

62. See, for example, Jim Seymour, "Send Out for Software," http://www.zdnet.com/pcmag/stories/reviews/0,6755, 2344646,00.html; Jim Seymour, "Which Apps Are Web Apps?" http://www.zdnet.com.pcmag/stories/reviews/0,6755,2344646, 00.html.

63. See http://www.corporate.ir-net/ireye/ir_site.zhtml? ticker+rhat&script=410&layout=9&item_id=46599; http://

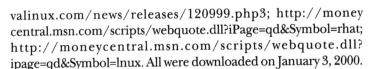

valinux.com/news/releases/120999.php3; http://money
central.msn.com/scripts/webquote.dll?iPage=qd&Symbol=rhat;
http://moneycentral.msn.com/scripts/webquote.dll?
ipage=qd&Symbol=lnux. All were downloaded on January 3, 2000.

64. Schmalensee Direct ¶ 102.

65. See Bernard Reddy, David Evans, and Albert Nichols, "Why
Does Microsoft Charge So Little for Windows?" http://www.
neramicrosoft.com/NERADocuments/Analyses/why_does_
micro.pdf. To obtain a profit-maximizing price in the range of
$65, the Justice Department's economist (Fisher) had to assume
an industry price elasticity of four and an average price for Intel-
compatible computer systems that is about half the actual average price. A price elasticity of four implies, preposterously, that a
10 percent increase in the price of personal computer systems
would result in a 40 percent decrease in industry sales.

66. Although Microsoft pricing information is confidential,
Microsoft's economist used a figure of $65 in public sessions as
the average price of Windows to original equipment manufacturers. The average price for PC hardware is about $1,700, and $65
is less than 4 percent of $1,700. See June 23, 1999 A.M. Session
Transcript, p. 14 (Schmalensee).

67. June 1, 1999, P.M. Session Transcript, p. 7 (Fisher).

68. See June 2, 1999, A.M. Session Transcript, pp. 6–7 (Fisher);
November 19, 1998, P.M. Session Transcript, pp. 33 (Warren-
Boulton). The government's economists appear to have adopted
that position in response to Schmalensee's testimony that the
threat of potential entry forced Microsoft to keep the price low.
Contrary to the view of the government's economists, limit pricing can be a rational strategy in the presence of network effects;
see Drew Fudenberg and Jean Tirole, "Producing under the
Threat of Entry by the Sole Supplier of a Network Good," a working paper, for further discussion. Prices below the short-run monopoly level might also make sense to stimulate growth in the
early stages of a market's development. But Microsoft's pricing
policy has been consistent for over a decade, and the government's
economists did not attempt an explanation along those lines.

69. Considerable testimony at the trial concerned the issue of
whether IE was integrated into, bolted to, welded to, or remov-
able from Windows. This testimony was relevant to the
government's claim that Microsoft had engaged in unlawful ty-

ing. Economists have identified few circumstances in which tying can harm consumers, and almost all of them believe that tying claims should be evaluated under the rule of reason to determine whether the anticompetitive costs outweigh the procompetitive benefits. Here, we focus on the narrow question of whether Microsoft's inclusion of browsing technology in Windows had the *effect* of foreclosing Netscape from distributing its browsing technology or of harming consumers.

70. See http://media.web.aol.com/media/press_view.cfm? release_num=100207&title=AOL%20SURPASSES%2019%20 MILLION%20MEMBERS.

71. See, for example, Frank H. Easterbrook, "Predatory Strategies and Counterstrategies," *University of Chicago Law Review* 48 (1981): 263–377; William J. Baumol and Janusz A. Ordover, "Use of Antitrust to Subvert Competition," *Journal of Law and Economics* 28 (1985): 247–65.

72. "Microsoft's zero pricing and vast spending for distribution of Internet Explorer . . . did not require for its anticompetitive effect an ability to raise the price of Internet Explorer in the future. It achieved an anticompetitive effect by perpetuating Microsoft's monopoly in the market *for another product,* the Windows operating system." Plaintiffs' Joint Proposed Conclusions of Law, p. 44 (emphasis in the original). June 2, 1999, A.M. Session Transcript, pp. 26–27 (Fisher).

73. As discussed in Richard Schmalensee, "Antitrust Issues in Schumpeterian Industries," *American Economic Review* 90 (2000): 172–96, that standard is problematic in industries, such as software, that are characterized by sequential races for category leadership.

74. CFOF ¶ 377. The e-mail says: "We set out on this mission 2 years ago to not let netscape dictate standards and control the browser api's [sic]. All evidence today says they don't." Ensuring that Internet standards are not under the control of any single firm is surely procompetitive and proconsumer.

75. June 22, 1999, P.M. Session Transcript, pp. 26–29 (Schmalensee).

76. June 21, 1999, P.M. Session Transcript, p. 90 (Schmalensee).

77. See Defendant's Exhibit 2440, p. AOL/N0341778.

78. See Schmalensee Direct, appendix F.

79. CFOF ¶ 239.

80. One of the merger due-diligence reports stated that they could "[e]stimate the client on 22% of OEM [original equipment manufacturer] shipments with minimal promotion." Defendant's Exhibit 2440, p. AOL/N0341778.

81. See Defendant's Exhibit 44 (an e-mail from Microsoft's Dan Rosen summarizing a meeting with Barksdale) and October 22, 1998, A.M. Session Transcript, pp. 73–75 (Barksdale).

82. This figure is based on NERA tabulations of MDC data. The percentages were higher for IE in both periods but grew much less rapidly.

83. See Defendant's Exhibit 2440, p. AOL/N0341778. Of the 160 million, 60 million are clearly labeled as downloads. Of the remaining 100 million distributed through "Exclusive Distribution Program" partners, presumably virtually all were also via downloads.

84. This is from NERA tabulations of MDC data.

85. This is from NERA tabulations of MDC data.

86. The Justice Department's economist, Professor Fisher, argued that Microsoft had raised Netscape's cost of distribution. He did not, however, attempt to show that Microsoft had engaged in a strategy of *raising rival's costs*, as that term is used in the economics literature, or that Microsoft's strategy had harmed consumers. June 1, 1999, P.M. Session Transcript, pp. 55–58 (Fisher). See also, for example, Thomas Krattenmaker and Steven Salop, "Anticompetitive Exclusion: Raising Rival's Costs to Achieve Power over Price," *Yale Law Journal* 96 (1986): 209.

87. These are from NERA tabulations of MDC data. The data used by the government tell a similar story among non-OLS subscribers for the shorter period that they cover (January 1997 through August 1998); Netscape's share declined only slightly until the fall of 1997, when IE 4 was released.

88. CFOF ¶ 93.

89. CFOF ¶ 109.

90. CFOF ¶ 93.

91. CFOF ¶ 120.

92. CFOF ¶ 98. Ironically, in light of the government's claims against Microsoft, the Native Signal Processing software was designed to take advantage of multimedia features that Intel had integrated into its processors—thereby replacing separate chips. Moreover, the multimedia extensions were proprietary to Intel,

and thus their use would have given it a major advantage over competitors that produced clones of its processors.

93. CFOF ¶ 408.

94. November 24, 1998, P.M. Session Transcript, pp. 40–45 (Warren-Boulton).

95. The government's economists argued that this cost is unlikely to be significant because many software vendors distribute any necessary new Windows code with their applications. But that is true only in the short run, for new elements of Windows.

96. Microsoft insisted only that end-users see the Windows desktop as designed by Microsoft on the first boot. Original equipment manufacturers could place—and promote—an icon that would change the screen on all subsequent boots to one designed by the manufacturer. See Ronald A. Cass, "Copyright, Licensing, and the First Screen," *University of Michigan Journal of Telecommunications & Technology* 35 (5) (1999): 35–71.

97. PPFOF ¶¶ 178, 300, 364.2, 406.3.2.

98. Schmalensee, "Antitrust Issues in Schumpeterian Industries."

99. Schmalensee Direct, table 13 (p. 256).

100. CFOF ¶¶ 33–34, 64–65.

101. Benjamin Cardozo, "Mr. Justice Holmes," *Harvard Law Review* 44 (1931): 682, 688.

102. Allchin Direct ¶¶ 262–71.

103. Franklin M. Fisher, John J. McGowan, and Joen Greenwood, *Folded, Spindled, and Mutilated: Economic Analysis and U.S. v. IBM* (Cambridge: MIT Press, 1983), p. 272.

Chapter 3: Misconceptions, Misdirection, and Mistakes

1. David S. Evans and Richard L. Schmalensee, "Be Nice to Your Rivals: How the Government Is Selling an Antitrust Case without Consumer Harm in *United States* v. *Microsoft.*"

2. We are indebted to Timothy Bresnahan and Wayne Dunham for comments on this chapter.

3. The Market Decisions Corporation survey data on which Evans and Schmalensee rely for propositions as to how consumers obtained their browsers are unreliable—as the court held in its findings of fact in *United States* v. *Microsoft* ¶371 (hereafter CFOF). On that very point, the unreliability is shown by the fact that users of Windows 98, all of whom received IE with that oper-

ating system, give inconsistent answers. For example, AOL users who were not accessing the Web and therefore not using an Internet browser to browse the Web were included in MDC's browser share data. (In note 21 of chapter 2, Evans and Schmalensee state that the court's ruling on that point ignored the fact that "the Justice Department's economist, Professor Franklin Fisher, . . . did not attempt to show that excluding those respondents would affect any conclusions." But, of course, excluding respondents with Windows 98 who did not know how they got their browser would not affect the numerical results as to the responses of others about how they obtained their browser. The point is that the survey questions asked are ambiguous on their face and that this is shown by the one case in which we know—approximately—what the true answers are.)

4. Evans and Schmalensee sneer (in note 21 of chapter 2) at our use of those data because "[n]either Netscape nor Microsoft used those data to measure browser shares." Evans and Schmalensee fail to mention that AOL used those data and that other sources confirm their results.

5. Franklin M. Fisher, John J. McGowan, and Joen Greenwood, *Folded, Spindled, and Mutilated: Economic Analysis and* U.S. *v.* IBM (Cambridge: MIT Press, 1983), p. 272.

6. Evans and Schmalensee describe those as "caffeine-fueled e-mails." That description is cute, but not a reason for disregarding them.

7. And it is not clear that Microsoft has even learned that. Some of the e-mails introduced at trial were written well after the trial had begun.

8. See, for example, Daniel L. Rubinfeld and John Hoven, "Innovation and Antitrust Enforcement," in Jerry Ellig, ed., *Dynamic Competition and Public Policy: Technology, Innovation, and Antitrust Issues* (New York: Cambridge University Press, 2000).

Chapter 4: Consumers Lose If Leading Firms Are Smashed for Competing

1. Franklin M. Fisher and Daniel L. Rubinfeld, "*United States* v. *Microsoft:* An Economic Analysis."

2. Court's findings of fact in *United States* v. *Microsoft* ¶ 412 (hereafter CFOF).

3. CFOF ¶ 109.

4. CFOF ¶¶ 93, 120.

5. Defendant's Exhibit 2440, p. AOL/N0341778.

6. For example, one of Professor Fisher's favorite phrases attributed to Bill Gates—"even if it makes no sense from a business standpoint"—is based on the deposition of Tim Schaaff of Apple, who reported hearing the phrase attributed to Gates from a Microsoft employee during negotiations (January 6, 1999, P.M. Session Transcript, pp. 71–72).

7. Fisher and Rubinfeld sometimes suggest that the real anticompetitive act was Microsoft's failure to offer an additional, browserless version of Windows, even though no other vendor offers such a crippled product. But Microsoft's refusal to offer a browser-free version would have reduced sales of Navigator only to the extent that consumers who wanted to use Netscape with Windows would only be willing to use the combination if the version of Windows lacked a browser. The government presented no evidence that *any* such individuals existed.

8. Defendant's Exhibit 2440, p. AOL/N0341778.

9. June 1, 1999, P.M. Session Transcript, p. 17.

10. June 2, 1999, A.M. Session Transcript, p. 31.

11. CFOF ¶ 371.

12. June 1, 1999, P.M. Session Transcript, pp. 22–24.

About the Authors

DAVID S. EVANS is senior vice president of the National Economic Research Associates, Inc., in Cambridge, Massachusetts. He is a consultant to the Microsoft Corporation, which supported preparation of his analysis in this volume.

FRANKLIN M. FISHER is the Jane Berkowitz Carlton and Dennis William Carlton Professor of Economics at the Massachusetts Institute of Technology. He was one of the U.S. government's economic witnesses at the Microsoft trial.

DANIEL L. RUBINFELD is the Robert L. Bridges Professor of Law and professor of economics at the University of California, Berkeley. During the Microsoft trial, he was deputy assistant attorney general for economics in the Antitrust Division of the U.S. Department of Justice and later a consultant to the U.S. government.

RICHARD L. SCHMALENSEE is dean and professor of management and economics at the Sloan School of Management of the Massachusetts Institute of Technology. He is a consultant to the Microsoft Corporation, which supported preparation of his analysis in this volume.

JOINT CENTER

www.ingramcontent.com/pod-product-compliance
Lightning Source LLC
Jackson TN
JSHW011939131224
75386JS00041B/1464

* 9 7 8 0 8 4 4 7 7 1 5 1 9 *